Dis

for studer

David Peaty

Oxford University Press

Oxford University Press
Walton Street, Oxford OX2 6DP

Oxford New York Toronto
Delhi Bombay Calcutta Madras Karachi
Petaling Jaya Singapore Hong Kong Tokyo
Nairobi Dar Es Salaam Cape Town
Melbourne Auckland

and associated companies in
Beirut Berlin Ibadan Nicosia

Oxford is a trade mark of Oxford University Press

ISBN 0 19 453261 5

© Oxford University Press 1984

First published 1984
Fourth impression 1987

The publishers would like to thank Oxfam for their
permission to use the advertisement on page 91
which is a modified version of an original.

The publishers would like to thank the following
for permission to use photographs and pictures:

Janet and Colin Bord; Camera Press; Christian
Aid; Format Photographers; Sally and Richard
Greenhill; International Freelance Library;
Network; Report; Rex Features; Ann Ronan
Picture Library; Frank Spooner Pictures.

Computerset by Promenade Graphics Ltd.,
Cheltenham
Printed in Hong Kong

Contents

To the student

This book has been written for learners of English who have already studied for several years and are interested in discussing topics of current interest such as hijacking and the environment. Each of the eighteen lessons consists of five parts: reading comprehension, listening comprehension, guided writing, role-playing discussion and language practice. When using this book, you should try to understand as much as possible without using a dictionary and without thinking about grammar. Remember to prepare each lesson very thoroughly before class and review it carefully afterwards.

At home

Reading comprehension

Read each passage three times. The first time, read quickly and try only to understand the general meaning of the passage. The second time, read slowly and carefully. Try to understand the passage in detail. Try to guess the meanings of words and phrases you do not know before looking them up in a dictionary. The third time, read the passage again quickly, trying to absorb as much as possible.

Next, try to answer the questions. If the passage is fairly short, you should be able to answer without looking at the text. If it is long, you may need to refer briefly to the text before answering each question.

Finally, consider the discussion questions carefully and prepare to present your own opinions in class.

Listening comprehension

Look up the meanings of the key words and phrases in your dictionary. Listen to each dialogue several times. The first time, listen without pausing and try to understand the general meaning. The second time, pause after each sentence and try to understand the exact meaning. The third time, look at the questions as you listen and pause each time you find an answer.

Don't try to reproduce the dialogue word for word or memorize it, but make notes of words and phrases you don't understand. Finally, consider the discussion questions carefully and prepare to present your own opinions in class.

Guided writing

Most of these exercises are based on a sample text on which your composition should be modelled. Make sure that you examine the sample text and read the instructions carefully before starting to write. Check your composition thoroughly before handing it to your teacher for correction.

Role-playing discussion

Consider the situation and roles carefully. You will later be asked to prepare and act out one of the roles in class.

Language practice

These exercises are designed to help you use important structures and expressions in daily conversation. Prepare them carefully before class and review them frequently afterwards.

In class

Your teacher will tell you exactly what to do, but you should keep the following points in mind. Try to answer comprehension questions without looking at your book. During the discussion in Parts 1, 2 and 3, try to express your own opinion clearly and listen carefully to the opinions expressed by your fellow students. In role-playing discussion, try to express the opinion which you think best fits the role you are playing, even if your own opinion is quite different. Other role-playing activities are based on the recorded dialogues and require you to act out dialogues which are approximately the same or to make up similar dialogues following the outlines provided in the book. In a few lessons, there are also role-playing activities based on reading passages which require you to ask and answer questions about the information given in the text. You will often be asked to do various activities on your own or with a partner without supervision from the teacher. Make the most of these opportunities to practise speaking English freely.

To the teacher

This book has been written for mature intermediate-level learners of English who require overall competence at a higher and more sophisticated level. It provides intensive practice in each of the fundamental skills through a variety of activities designed to maximize student involvement and motivation. Each lesson focusses on a specific theme and consists of five sections:

Part 1 is aimed at reading comprehension and consists of a text, questions on meaning and vocabulary, and outlines for discussion or role-play.

Part 2 focusses on listening comprehension based on a recorded dialogue (a transcript of which can be found at the back of the book), comprehension questions, and outlines for discussion or role-play.

Part 3 generally consists of a short reading passage on which guided-writing assignments are based.

Part 4 provides outlines for creative role-playing, generally in the form of a group discussion or problem-solving activity.

Part 5 contains exercises designed for further practice of structures and functions.

Each section may be dealt with in various ways, depending on class size, available time, student background and so on. You may find the following suggestions helpful.

Reading comprehension

Students should read the text carefully before the lesson and prepare answers to the questions and vocabulary exercises. Although the texts are intended for silent reading, you may wish to read them or have them read aloud in class before asking the questions. Since the texts are usually rather complex, students may be unable to answer with books closed. In large classes, it may be useful to have the students ask and answer the questions again in pairs.

Listening comprehension

Students should listen to the recording carefully before the lesson and prepare their answers to the questions. They should study the key words (looking them up in a dictionary if necessary) before listening for the first time. They should not attempt to understand the dialogues word for word but should try instead to pick out the general meaning. The recording should be played several times in class before you ask individual students to answer questions orally. Since many of the dialogues are long and complex, you may need to stop the tape after each utterance or paragraph to ask specific questions. Having obtained the correct answers, you may wish to play the cassette again without stopping to allow the students to find out how much they can now understand.

Discussion

Most reading and listening-comprehension activities are followed by discussion outlines. Students should consider the questions carefully before class and be ready to express their opinions. In small classes, each question may be directed to several or all of the students; in larger classes, discussion will have to be done in groups or pairs. Students should not be corrected during discussion but you should make notes of errors to be commented on afterwards.

Role-play

Most listening-comprehension activities are followed by role-playing outlines. These require pairs of students to reproduce an approximation of the original dialogue, using the comprehension questions or given outline as a guide, or to make up similar dialogues using the given outline or their own ideas. It should not be necessary for students to memorize the original dialogue word for word. A few dialogues should be heard and corrected before the class divides into pairs for role-play. Students should exchange roles in order to practise both parts in a dialogue. There are also a few role-playing activities based on reading passages (Units 8, 16 and 18). These require students to ask and answer questions about the text and should be dealt with in the same way as other role-playing activities.

Guided writing

The writing assignments should be explained at the end of each class and done for homework and handed to you for correction. In most cases, the text used in this section will also serve as the basis for further discussion in class.

Role-playing discussion

The situation should be explained carefully and then roles chosen or assigned. Students without roles may act as chairpersons or secretaries (making notes, looking up words, etc.). Large classes should be divided into small groups in order to give everyone a chance to speak. Students will need ten or fifteen minutes to prepare their ideas before discussion begins. Notes should be very brief. During discussion, shy students should be encouraged to speak out and more extrovert students should be discouraged from interrupting. Correction of mistakes should be done after the discussion is over.

Language practice

Most of these exercises may be done orally with books closed. This is not possible with some of the more complex structural drills, however. Each exercise should first be performed by selected students for correction or approval by the teacher. Then students should do the exercises simultaneously, alone (structural exercises) or in pairs (functional exercises). Many of the structural exercises are also suitable for guided-writing practice.

Photographs and statistics

These are intended to provide a stimulus to preliminary discussion. You may either ask factual questions such as 'What is happening in this picture?' or opinion-oriented ones such as 'What do you think of this situation/these statistics?'. It is better not to let the discussion become too involved at this stage, however.

Notes on grammar have been excluded in accordance with the principle that structure, like functions and vocabulary, is best learned in context. Students should be encouraged to try to guess the meanings of unfamiliar words before looking them up in a dictionary. However, the lessons tend to become progressively more difficult in terms of content and theme and eventually the dictionary may become indispensible.

In conclusion, it should be stressed that every unit must be prepared thoroughly before class and reviewed periodically later.

1 A place to live

Part 1

New York City, with over seven million inhabitants, is one of the largest cities in the world. With such a vast population, it inevitably suffers from an acute housing shortage. Property is extremely expensive to buy so ordinary people have to live in rented apartments. Such apartments, however, are in very short supply.

One reason for this is the system of strict rent stabilization which was intended to protect poor tenants from unscrupulous landlords but has instead reduced the supply of low-cost housing. Landlords, faced with rising maintenance costs which they are not permitted to pass on to tenants, frequently allow their buildings to become derelict and abandon them. When the official tenants leave, squatters move in and occupy the tenements until they are evicted by the police. Finally the buildings are pulled down and replaced by expensive condominiums, which are more attractive to investors.

As a result, it is becoming harder and harder for people with low incomes to find vacant apartments. The city government makes up for this to some extent by building apartments at public expense but its efforts are limited by lack of funds.

Reading comprehension

1 What is the population of New York City?
2 Why do ordinary people live in rented apartments?
3 Is it easy to find such apartments?
4 Are rents very high? Why (not)?
5 What was the purpose of rent stabilization?
6 What effect has it had?
7 Why do some landlords abandon their buildings?
8 What happens to the buildings after the official tenants leave?
9 Who removes the squatters?
10 When the buildings are pulled down, what replaces them?
11 Why do investors prefer expensive condominiums?
12 How does this affect the supply of low-cost housing?
13 Does the city government make up for this? How?
14 Why doesn't it build more apartments?

Discussion

Which is the largest city in your country?
What is its population?
Does it suffer from housing shortages?
Are rents stabilized? Should they be? Why (not)?
What should city governments do about housing problems?
Would you rather live in a large city or a small town? Why?

Vocabulary

1 Explain the meanings of these words and phrases as they are used in the text:

in short supply	condominiums
maintenance costs	attractive
derelict	at public expense
squatters	

2 Choose the words or phrases most similar in meaning to the
following as used in the reading passage:

over (a) about (b) more than (c) less than
inhabitants (a) natives (b) populations (c) residents
inevitably (a) unavoidably (b) naturally (c) obviously
acute (a) sharp (b) severe (c) chronic
unscrupulous (a) greedy (b) ruthless (c) lacking in moral
    principles
permitted (a) allowed (b) forgiven (c) made
abandon (a) leave (b) reject (c) waste
evicted (a) ejected (b) transferred (c) arrested
vacant (a) empty (b) spacious (c) cheap
makes up for (a) provides for (b) allows for (c) compensates for

Part 2

Listen to the recording of a dialogue between a landlord and a
tenant.

Listening comprehension

1 What bad news does the landlord have to tell his tenant?
2 How does the tenant react?
3 Why does the landlord insist?
4 Why is this unreasonable?
5 Will the landlord repair the apartment?
6 Does the tenant agree to sign a new lease?
7 Why not?
8 What will the landlord do about this?

Role-play

Working in pairs, make up and act out similar dialogues.

Discussion

If the tenant cannot afford to pay the new rent, should he leave?
Why (not)?
What would you do if you were the tenant/the landlord?
Is it reasonable to increase the rent by 25%? Why (not)?
Do situations like this occur in your country?

Part 3

Guided writing

The landlord had to notify his tenant in writing. This is what he wrote.

---

26 April 19..

Dear Mr. Cooper,

We regret to inform you that the apartment which you now occupy is to be rented to a new tenant next month. We must therefore ask you to leave by the end of this month. If you fail to do so, we will apply for a court eviction order.

Yours sincerely,

Paul Rachman

Write Mr. Cooper's letter of reply in which he refuses to leave, giving the following reasons:

1 He and his family have lived in the apartment for over two years.
2 They have nowhere else to live.
3 They need at least three months in which to find another place to live.
4 Mr. Rachman has no legal right to evict them.

Part 4

Apartment for rent.
Call evenings 2187645.

Mr. Cooper sees the above advertisement in a local newspaper and telephones to find out:

if the apartment is still available (it is)
its location (Brooklyn)
the rent (450 dollars a month)
the size (bedroom, kitchen, bathroom)
the age (built 45 years ago)

He then arranges to see the apartment at a mutually convenient time.

Role-play

Make up a dialogue to fit this situation. Begin like this:

Landlord: 2187645.

Cooper: Hello. I believe you advertised an apartment for rent. Is it still available?

Part 5

Language practice

Change the following sentences as shown in the examples.

1 It is expensive to buy property.
   Property is expensive to buy.

   It is hard to find cheap apartments.
   It is dangerous to live in abandoned buildings.
   It is difficult to evict tenants.
   It is profitable to build condominiums.
   It is expensive to maintain old apartments.

2 It is hard to find vacant apartments.
   It is becoming harder and harder to find vacant apartments.

   It is profitable to build condominiums.
   It is easy to find new tenants.
   It is necessary to change the system.
   It is hard to raise rents.
   It is expensive to live in the city.

3 In the dialogue, the landlord begins his unpleasant demand with:
   I'm sorry to have to tell you this but . . .

   The tenant begins his rejection with:
   I'm afraid I can't agree to that.

   Use these expressions to make and reject the following demands.

   Your rent has been increased.
   Your wages have been cut.
   Your vacation will have to be postponed.
   You will have to work overtime tonight.

2 Education

Part 1

After rising steadily for almost a century, standards of education in the public schools of Europe and North America have levelled off and, in the opinion of many parents and employers, are actually falling. More and more children are leaving school with little more than a basic knowledge of reading, writing and arithmetic, and illiteracy is becoming a social problem once again. With dropout rates of twenty-seven per cent in high schools and fifty per cent in colleges, the American education system is clearly in trouble; European dropout rates, though lower than those of the U.S., are rising too.

Various factors have been blamed for the apparent decline in educational standards. Some people say that overcrowding and lack of discipline are major factors. Others maintain that subjects like art and drama have been overemphasized at the expense of more practical subjects. The negative influence of television is frequently mentioned as a reason for growing illiteracy. Many teachers and principals, however, insist that the problem is not of falling standards but of rising expectations on the part of parents and employers.

Whether or not standards in public schools are actually falling, many parents feel that the only way to secure a good education for their children is to send them to private schools, which generally have smaller classes and stricter discipline. The popularity of such schools is growing steadily, despite the high tuition fees. In the United States, for example, eleven per cent of all school children attend private schools; in France, over sixteen per cent do so.

Reading comprehension

1 For how long were standards of education rising?
2 Who believes they are falling now?
3 How is this related to the problem of illiteracy?
4 How many children drop out of American high schools each year?
5 What organizational factors may have caused standards to fall?
6 According to some people, which subjects have not received enough emphasis?
7 Does television have a good or bad influence on literacy?
8 What do many teachers and principals think the cause of the problem is?
9 Why do many parents send their children to private schools?

10 What are the advantages of private schools?
11 What is the biggest disadvantage?

Discussion

Are schools in your country overcrowded? If so, why?
Is lack of discipline in schools a problem in your country?
If so, what should be done about it?
Do you think television has a good or bad influence on literacy?
Why?
Would you rather attend a public school or a private school? Why?
Which of the following subjects should receive most emphasis?
Why?

native language	history	religion
foreign languages	music	physical education
mathematics	economics	religious education
science	art	
geography	sports	

Vocabulary

Choose the words or phrases most similar in meaning to the
following as used in the reading passage:

levelled off (a) stopped rising (b) become equal (c) started falling
illiteracy (a) ignorance (b) lack of intelligence (c) inability to read
    and write properly
apparent (a) obvious (b) seeming (c) doubtful
discipline (a) control (b) authority (c) rule
practical (a) basic (b) useful (c) important
frequently (a) often (b) sometimes (c) generally
despite (a) although (b) because of (c) in spite of
fees (a) prices (b) costs (c) charges

Part 2

Read through the following list of key words and phrases before
listening to the recording of an interview with the Commissioner of
the Department of Education:

equality of opportunity	depressed areas
realize (his/her) potential	abolished
unfair advantage	financial burden
budget	

Listening comprehension

1 Is there equality of opportunity in education in the Commissioner's opinion?
2 Do rich children have an unfair advantage?
3 What does success depend on, according to the Commissioner?
4 Why do some private schools have higher standards?
5 Why hasn't the Government raised the standard of public education in depressed areas?
6 Does the Commissioner think that private schools should be abolished or encouraged? Why?

Role-play

In pairs, conduct a similar interview on education in your country. Find out:

if there is equality of opportunity in education
if private education gives rich children an advantage
if private schools have higher standards
if your partner thinks private schools should be abolished

Part 3

The American Education System

In the United States, education is compulsory from the age of five or six to fifteen or sixteen, depending on the state. Children generally study for eight years in an elementary school and three years in a junior high (or middle) school, although many states have different systems. After graduating from high school, students who wish to go to college must pass entrance examinations. College degree programs generally last for four years.

Discussion

In what ways does the education system of your country differ from that of the U.S.?
Which system is better? Why?

Guided writing

Write a similar description of the education system of your country.

Part 4
Role-play

Although most high-school students want to go to college, it seems that a college education is not always advantageous. Read the interview below and conduct similar ones in pairs, using your own ideas.

Interviewer What did you major in at college?

Dropout Greek literature.

Interviewer When did you graduate?

Dropout Twelve years ago.

Interviewer Did you manage to find a job?

Dropout Yes. Several, in fact. I worked in a restaurant, washing dishes. I almost became a bus driver, but I failed the driving test . . .

Interviewer Why didn't you find a job related to your college studies?

Dropout Because there aren't any. Employers don't seem to be interested in Greek literature.

Discussion

What kind of employment could a Greek literature major find?
Is it better to study more practical subjects?
Which subjects do you consider to be most practical? Why?
If you could choose quite freely, which subjects would you most like to study at college? Why?
Do you consider the main purpose of education to be:

    to prepare oneself for one's future career
    to develop one's personality and intellect
    to enjoy oneself
    any other purpose?

Part 5
Language practice

Change the following sentences as shown in the examples.

1 They send them to private schools although the fees are high.
They send them to private schools despite the high fees.

    I like my job although the wages are low.
    We played football although the weather was bad.
    He continued to smile although the news was bad.
    He is popular although his ideas are old-fashioned.
    We enjoyed our meal although the service was bad.

2 What do you mean?
  It depends what you mean.

  Who are you?
  Where do you live?
  How much money do you have?
  Which school did you attend?
  When did you graduate?

3 I'm rich.
  It makes no difference whether you are rich or not.

  I went to university.
  I studied Greek literature.
  I have an honors degree.
  My references are good.
  I graduated from a famous university.

3 Public transportation

Part 1

The National Railways have been losing money for years, but until recently nobody paid much attention to the problem. The deficits were covered by government subsidies which were financed out of general taxation.

This year, however, the railways made a record loss and leaders of the Opposition demanded that the Government take action to reduce the deficit. The Prime Minister, anticipating an angry reaction from taxpayers, ordered that a commission be set up to find ways of making the railways more efficient.

The Commission's report, which was published three days ago, showed that most of the losses were made on local lines with few passengers. It also indicated that the National Railways had far too many employees. The Commission recommended that unprofitable lines be closed and that the work force be reduced.

The Government has already accepted these recommendations in principle and is now considering which lines to close and how to trim the work force. Although there have been no official announcements yet, it is believed that over forty lines will be closed and that no new workers will be hired for several years.

Reading comprehension

1 What is the National Railways' problem?
2 How were the deficits covered?
3 Why did people start to pay attention to the problem this year?
4 What did Opposition leaders want the Government to do?
5 What did the Prime Minister do?
6 Why did he do that?
7 Why should taxpayers be angry?
8 What did the Commission's report show?
9 What did the Commission advise the Government to do?
10 Will the Government follow the advice of the Commission?
11 Has it announced its plans officially?
12 What will it probably do to make the railways more efficient?

Vocabulary

Choose the words or phrases most similar in meaning to the following as used in the reading passage:

deficits (a) payments (b) costs (c) losses
subsidies (a) financial contributions (b) loans (c) taxes
record (a) biggest (b) bigger than ever before (c) extraordinary
anticipating (a) hoping (b) expecting (c) fearing
efficient (a) profitable (b) useful (c) cheap
local (a) nearby (b) regional (c) rural
reduced (a) cut (b) dismissed (c) fallen
trim (a) improve (b) economize (c) reduce

Part 2

Read through the key words before listening to the recording of a dialogue between Mr. Preston, a Government spokesman, and Mrs. Randolph, the representative of a group campaigning against the closure of local lines.

congested   deserted   essential   responsibility

Listening comprehension

1 What will happen, according to Mrs. Randolph, if local lines are closed?
2 Why does Mr. Preston think they should be closed?
3 Does Mrs. Randolph think it is necessary for railways to make a profit? Why (not)?
4 Who does she think is responsible for public transportation?
5 What is Mr. Preston's opinion?
6 What will train services be replaced by?

Role-play

In pairs, act out this dialogue.

Discussion

Are the railways in your country owned by the state or by private companies?
Are they profitable? Why (not)?
Should unprofitable lines be closed? Why (not)? How could they be made more profitable?
Would you rather travel by train or by car? Why?

Part 3

Weston is located about 80 kilometers west of the capital city. It has a population of about 150,000, many of whom commute to the capital every day. Most of them go by car, so the main road is very congested, especially during the rush hour. There are long traffic jams and sometimes accidents. It is possible to go by train, but fares are high and connections with the main line at Easton are bad, so the trains are usually half empty.

Guided writing

Study the above description of Weston and its transportation facilities and then write a similar description of the town in which you live or were born and the transportation services available there.

Part 4

Role-playing discussion

The Government has decided to close the Weston line and to build a new highway to Easton. People who will be affected by the plan are holding a meeting to decide whether the town should support or oppose it. Allocate the following roles to students in the class.

Alan Moore, whose bus company operates services from Weston to Easton and the capital city.

Linda Craig, an executive who commutes to the capital every day and has no driver's licence.

Helen Fisher, spokeswoman for the local ratepayers' association, whose members all have cars

Joe Adams, representative of a village which will be destroyed to make way for the highway.

Henry Smith, chief of Weston Police Force, who is concerned about traffic jams and accidents on the old road.

Gordon Mitchell, secretary of the Weston chapter of the rail union, whose members may lose their jobs.

Donald Bell, a retired principal, who will chair the meeting.

Students without specific roles should make up the rest of the audience and are free to criticize/support the arguments presented to them.

Part 5

Language practice

Change the following sentences as shown in the examples.

1   Unprofitable lines should be closed.
    They recommended that unprofitable lines be closed.

    Deficits should be reduced.
    A commission should be set up.
    Inefficient workers should be fired.
    Train timetables should be revised.
    Train fares should be increased.

2   The Government must take action.
    They demanded that the Government take action.

    The Minister must resign.
    The Government must build more railways.
    Trains must be more punctual.
    Employees must work harder.
    A no-smoking policy must be introduced.

3   I'm tired.
    I suggest (that) you go to bed.

    My new car won't start.
    It's going to rain.
    I want to learn English.
    My job is very boring.
    I have a bad toothache.

4   Agreement may be expressed in the following ways:
    I agree.
    I think so too.

    Disagreement may be expressed in the following ways:
    I disagree.
    I'm afraid I don't agree.

    Agree or disagree with the following statements, using one of the above expressions:
    Railroads are an essential public service.
    Unprofitable lines should be closed.
    Transportation should not be subsidized by taxpayers.
    Train fares should be increased.
    The Government should build more highways.

4 Health

Life expectancy rates: average ages of death in developed and developing countries. Source: World Development Report 1983.

Highest expectancy		Lowest expectancy	
1 Japan Sweden	77	1 Afghanistan	37
		2 Somalia	39

2 Netherlands
  France
  Norway
  Switzerland
	76	3 Angola	42

		4 Lao Por
		  Guinea
		  Central African Republic
		  Yemen Republic
			43

3 Hong Kong
  Finland
  Canada
  U.S.A.
  Denmark
	75	5 Malawi
		  Upper Volta
		  Senegal
		  Mauritania
			44

4 Greece
  Spain
  Italy
  New Zealand
  U.K.
	74		

5 Israel	73		

Part 1

The most common causes of death among western people are heart disease and cancer. Thanks to recent medical research, new effective drugs have been developed and surgical techniques have been improved. But even greater progress has been made in the field of prevention. The old proverb "prevention is the surest form of cure" has never been more relevant than now. Having identified the causes of most common diseases, we are now able to prevent them.

Heart disease is caused by obesity, stress and smoking. It can often be avoided simply by eating the right food and by getting plenty of exercise. Many types of cancer are caused by dietary factors and may be prevented by maintaining a healthy, balanced diet. Lung cancer is generally caused by living and working in a polluted environment and by smoking. It may be avoided by changing one's environment and by quitting smoking. Prevention is not only the surest form of cure, it is also the cheapest!

Reading comprehension

1 What are the most common causes of death among western people?
2 What are the benefits of recent medical research?
3 In which field has the most progress been made?
4 What does the old proverb say?
5 Is it relevant today? Why?
6 What causes heart disease?
7 How can it be avoided?
8 How may people avoid types of cancer which are caused by diet?
9 How do people generally get lung cancer?
10 How can it be avoided?
11 What are the advantages of prevention of disease?

Vocabulary

Choose the word or phrase most similar in meaning to the following as used in the reading passage:

improved (a) increased (b) developed (c) made better
field (a) area (b) subject (c) study
proverb (a) saying (b) idiom (c) expression
relevant (a) true (b) accurate (c) significant
obesity (a) fatness (b) heaviness (c) overeating
cure (a) remedy (b) treatment (c) medicine

Part 2

Listen to the recording of a dialogue between two people at a party.

Listening comprehension

1 How old is Mrs. Norfolk?
2 How old does she look?
3 What is her secret?
4 What does she eat every day?
5 Has she ever been sick?

Role-play

Working in pairs, make up and act out similar dialogues.

Discussion

Are you healthy? Have you ever been sick?
What should people do in order to stay healthy?
What do you think of Mrs. Norfolk's diet?
Have you ever eaten granola, tofu or brown rice?
What other kinds of food are good for health? Why?
What kinds of food and drink are bad for health? Why?

Part 3

How to prepare Spinach Tofu Soup

First, cut a large amount of spinach and a small onion into tiny pieces and fry them in butter for about three minutes.

Next, dissolve two or three cubes of vegetable soup stock in boiling water. After cooling, mix it with the spinach and onion in a food mixer.

Finally, put the mixture in a saucepan and add some tofu and a pinch of salt. Heat it until it starts to boil and then stir in milk or fresh cream.

Guided writing

Study the above recipe carefully and then write:

(a) a similar recipe for your favorite dish or
(b) instructions on how to make an omelette or a cup of tea.

Part 4

Role-playing discussion

Your local authorities are planning to add fluoride to the city water supply. Citizens are holding a meeting to decide whether to accept or oppose the plan. Some believe it will ensure that everyone has healthy teeth and will save on dental expenses. Others believe that they should have the right to choose individually and that they can use fluoride toothpaste and cut down on sugar if they want to protect their teeth. Some even believe that fluoride causes cancer.

Discuss the issue under the direction of a chairman/woman and then take a vote on it.

Part 5

Language practice

Change the following sentences as shown in the examples.

1 They have made progress.
Progress has been made.

They have developed new drugs.
They have improved surgical techniques.
They have eliminated smallpox.
They have identified the causes of diseases.
They have conquered cancer.

2 We can avoid heart disease.
Heart disease can be avoided.

We may prevent cancer.
We should ban smoking.
We must protect the environment.
We should control pollution.
We can improve our health.

3 You can avoid heart disease if you eat the right food.
You can avoid heart disease by eating the right food.

They can control pollution if they make strict laws.
They can prevent lung cancer if they ban smoking.
We can improve our health if we get plenty of exercise.
You can relax if you do yoga.
We can save money if we prevent disease.

4 When we do not hear or understand what someone has just said, we often say:

Excuse me?
I'm sorry, what did you say?
Sorry, could you say that again?

When only a word or two were not clear, we indicate this as follows:

I eat tofu every day.
Excuse me? What do you eat every day?

I met Mrs. Norfolk.
I beg your pardon? Who did you meet?

In the following sentences, one word (. . .) is not clear to the listener. Use the above technique to get the speaker to repeat the indistinct word.

Mr. . . . had an accident yesterday.
He fell off his . . . .
He'll be in the hospital for . . . weeks.
I sent him a . . . today.
I can't go and see him because . . . .

5 Advertising

Part 1

Since the early 1950s, private companies have been spending more and more on advertising in the mass media. Although some advertisements provide information of public interest, it is clear that most are aimed at sales promotion. In some cases, rival products which are almost identical are advertised at great expense. Many consumers complain that such promotional advertising is wasteful and pushes up prices. Advertising executives, however, maintain that by advertising, they can increase sales and thus gain economies of large-scale production which are passed on to consumers. However justified this expenditure may be from the viewpoint of private enterprise, it is certainly remarkable that in many capitalist countries, more money is spent on advertising than on schools or hospitals.

Reading comprehension

1 What is the main aim of advertising?
2 How do consumers feel about promotional advertising?
3 How can advertising help to reduce prices?
4 Is promotional advertising justifiable from a social point of view?
   Why (not)?

Discussion

What do you think are the most effective types of advertisements? Why?
Can you give examples of (a) advertisements which provide information of public interest (b) identical rival products?
Do you think advertising raises or lowers prices? Why?

Vocabulary

1 Explain the meanings of the following words and phrases as used in the reading passage:

   the early 1950s
   mass media
   sales promotion
   economies of large-scale production
   passed on to consumers

2 Find words or phrases in the reading passage which mean:

directed at
surprising
competing
exactly the same
spending
people who buy or use goods

Part 2

Read through the following key words and phrases before listening to the recording of an interview with the president of an advertising agency:

existing products	mislead
discover latent needs	imply
junk food	nutritious
consumers' associations	anticipate

Listening comprehension

1 Why do large firms spend so much money on advertising?
2 Do advertisers persuade people to buy things which they don't need?
3 How did toothpaste commercials help many people?
4 What do some consumers' associations say about junk food commercials?
5 Does Ms. Sellars agree? Why (not)?
6 What trends in advertising over the next ten years does Ms. Sellars anticipate? Why?

Role-play

Conduct a similar interview to find out:

why so much money is spent on advertising
if advertisers try to persuade people to buy things they don't need
if harmful products are advertised
if junk food commercials are misleading
the prospects for the advertising industry over the next ten years

Discussion

To what extent does advertising influence your purchasing decisions?

Can you find examples of (a) advertising of harmful products
(b) misleading advertisements?

Do you think such advertisements should be prohibited? If so, why?

Part 3

23, Morris Avenue,
Langton,
Devon

16 May 19 ..

The Manager
ABC Chemical Company Ltd.
Westford Street
London

Dear Sir,

    Last month, I bought a bottle of 'Nulife Shampoo',
manufactured by your company, after seeing it advertised on
television. I used it three times, expecting that it would make
my hair lively and attractive, as claimed in the television
commercial. On the contrary, however, my hair became dry
and lifeless. Worse still, it has started to go grey in places.

    I therefore request that you refund the cost of the shampoo
and compensate me for the damage to my hair. If you fail to do
so, I will make a formal complaint to the Advertising
Standards Bureau.

    Yours,

      Mabel Cummings

Guided writing

Study the above letter of complaint carefully and then write a similar
letter to the ABC Chemical Company about one of the following
items:

(a) cough medicine which irritated your throat and made your
cough worse

(b) toothpaste which turned your teeth yellow and caused tooth
decay.

Part 4

Role-playing discussion

Members of a parliamentary commission are meeting to discuss a proposal to abolish commercial television.

If the proposal is accepted, private television companies will be closed and the State Broadcasting Company, which is subsidized out of general taxation, will have a broadcasting monopoly.

Some members are in favor of the proposal, while others are against it. Here are some of the arguments which might be used.

For	Against
Commercials are wasteful and inflationary	State broadcasting monopoly could be used for propaganda
Harmful products are advertised	Commercials stimulate the economy
Commercial T.V. programs are in bad taste	Commercials are needed to inform the public about new products
Commercials often mislead the public	Commercials subsidize television programs

Part 5

Language practice

1 It is remarkable that . . .
  It is remarkable that so much money is spent on advertising.

  Make sentences beginning with the following phrases:

  It is surprising that . . .
  It is a shame that . . .
  It seems that . . .
  It is unfortunate that . . .
  It is obvious that . . .

2 Change the following sentences as shown in the example.

  They say that advertising is wasteful.
  It is said that advertising is wasteful.

  They know that a lot of money is spent.
  They believe that advertising pushes up prices.
  They think that the advertising industry will continue to grow.
  They hope that misleading commercials will be prohibited.

3 Notice how the reporter in the recorded interview softens his
criticism of advertising in the following sentence:
Surely many harmful products are also advertised, aren't they?

Do the same with these statements:

Advertising pushes up prices.
Many commercials mislead consumers.
Advertising is wasteful.
You persuade people to buy things which they don't need.
Consumers cannot help being influenced by commercials.

6 Hijack

Hijacked Boeing 707 at Damascus Airport.

Part 1

Editorial

Yesterday evening, a National Airways plane carrying two hundred and thirty-four passengers was hijacked by a young man who threatened to shoot the pilot unless he was given a million dollars ransom. The Government paid the money and the incident ended without loss of life.

The prompt decision of the Government to pay the ransom no doubt saved the lives of the passengers and crew members who would have died if the hijacker had carried out his threat to kill the pilot. It sets a dangerous precedent, however. By giving in so easily, the Government has encouraged hijacking. Many people feel that the authorities need not have handed over the money after the plane landed and that the hijacker should have been arrested on the spot, instead of being allowed to leave with the money.

Another matter of great concern is the laxity of airport security checks. The hijacker should not have been allowed to board the plane with a gun. If the security officers had searched him properly, they would have found his weapon and the whole incident would have been avoided. Airport security must be tightened up immediately.

Reading comprehension

1 Who did the Government pay a million dollars to? Why?
2 What would the hijacker have done if his demand had been refused?
3 What would have happened to the passengers and crew members if the hijacker had shot the pilot?
4 Was anyone killed in the incident?
5 Does the writer of this editorial approve of the Government's decision to pay the ransom?
6 What harmful consequences may follow as a result of this decision?
7 What do many people think the Government should have done?
8 Why didn't the airport security officers find the hijacker's gun?
9 What would have happened if they had found it?
10 How can future hijacking incidents be prevented?

Vocabulary

Choose the word or phrase most similar in meaning to the following as used in the reading passage:

incident (a) accident (b) affair (c) problem
prompt (a) quick (b) sudden (c) hasty
no doubt (a) definitely (b) probably (c) presumably
carried out (a) obeyed (b) fulfilled (c) completed
on the spot (a) immediately (b) at the scene of the crime (c) as soon
    as the plane landed
laxity (a) severity (b) gentleness (c) carelessness
tightened up (a) made more powerful (b) made stricter (c) made
    more efficient

Part 2
Listening comprehension
Listen to the recording of a meeting between the president of the
country in which the hijacked plane landed and the ambassador of
the country to which the plane belonged. Answer the following
questions.

1 Why has the ambassador come to see the president?
2 Will the hijacker and the money be returned? Why (not)?
3 Who will give the ambassador further information?

Role-play
Working in pairs, make up and act out similar dialogues.

Part 3

NEWS REPORT   Plane Hijacked

Yesterday evening at 8 p.m. a National Airways plane bound
for Rome with 234 passengers aboard was hijacked by a young
man armed with a gun. He demanded one million dollars
ransom and a guarantee of safe conduct and threatened to kill
the pilot unless his demands were met. The Government
immediately agreed to pay the ransom. The plane landed
somewhere in North Africa and the hijacker was given the
money. He got off the plane and was escorted away by airport
officials. The plane then continued its journey, arriving in
Rome fifteen hours behind schedule.

Role-play

In pairs, act out the interview between the reporter who wrote the news story above and an official of National Airways. Ask and answer the questions about:

the time of the hijack   his threat
the number of passengers   the Government's reaction
the destination of the plane   the place where the plane landed
the hijacker   the fate of the hijacker
his demands   the time the plane arrived in Rome

Guided writing

Write a similar report about a hijack based on the following details:

plane World Airways jumbo jet
destination New York
number of passengers 173
time of hijack yesterday afternoon at 3 p.m.
hijackers three young men
weapons swords
demands release of their leader from a New York prison

Continue the report using your own ideas.

Part 4

Study this list of previous hijacks:

1 A Japan Airlines jumbo jet was hijacked to Dacca, Bangla Desh.
   The Japanese government paid a ransom of six million dollars and
   released a number of convicted terrorists from prison.
2 A Lufthansa jet was hijacked to Mogadishu, Somalia. German
   commandos attacked the plane, killed the hijackers and rescued
   the hostages.
3 An Israeli plane was hijacked to Entebbe, Uganda. Israeli
   commandos killed the hijackers and rescued the hostages. Three
   hostages, one commando and twenty Ugandan soldiers were
   killed, in addition to the hijackers.
4 A Pakistan International Airways jet was hijacked to Kabul,
   Afghanistan. The Pakistan government, after more than a week of
   negotiating, released a number of political prisoners from Pakistan
   jails.
5 A Garuda Airways plane was hijacked to Bangkok, Thailand.
   Indonesian soldiers attacked the plane. Four of the hijackers were
   killed and one was captured. One passenger was killed in the
   crossfire.

6 A China Airlines plane was hijacked from Shanghai to South
   Korea. The hijackers released the passengers and asked for
   political asylum. It was granted.

Close your book and report to the rest of the class/group on one of
the above incidents. Add further details (true or imaginary) and give
your opinion on how the incident should have been handled.

Discussion

If you had been responsible for deciding what the Government
should have done in each of these situations, what would your
decision have been? Why?

Is the number of passengers or size of ransom significant in deciding
whether or not to give in to the hijacker's demands?
How can hijacking be prevented in the future?
What kind of punishment should hijackers be given?
Can hijacking be justified under any circumstances?

Role-playing discussion

An airplane belonging to one of your country's civil airlines has just
been hijacked. It is carrying 240 passengers, including your vice-
president. The hijacker has demanded a million dollars ransom and
the release from prison of his five terrorist friends. The plane will
land in Moronia, which has no diplomatic relations with your
country but might agree to return the hijacker if you offer a large
amount of economic aid. You, the Government's chief advisors,
must decide what should be done. The possibilities include:

   giving in to the hijacker's demands
   rejecting his demands
   negotiating with him to accept the money without the release of
       his friends from prison
   making a deal with Moronia
   sending commandos to shoot the hijacker

Discuss these possibilities in groups and reach a consensus.

Part 5

Language practice

1 Say what *would have* happened using the given cues.
The hijacker didn't kill the pilot. (plane crash)
If the hijacker had killed the pilot, the plane would have crashed.

The security officers did not search the hijacker. (find the gun)
The Government did not send any marines. (kill the hijacker)
The hijacker did not fall asleep. (passengers escape)
The passengers did not know about the hijack. (be worried)
The hijacker was not arrested. (be sent to prison)

2 Imagine what *would have* happened.
The Government gave in to the hijacker.
If the Government had not given in to the hijacker, he would have killed the pilot.

The hijacker spoke English.
The plane had enough fuel.
The North African country agreed to accept the plane.
The plane landed safely.
The pilot stayed calm.

3 Make criticisms based on the following statements.
   a The security officers did not search him.
      They should have searched him.

      They did not find his gun.
      The pilot did not attack the hijacker.
      The Government did not send the marines.
      The hijacker was not arrested.
      The North African country did not return the money.

   b They let him get away.
      They should not have let him get away.

      They gave him the money.
      They agreed to his conditions.
      They kept their promise.
      They encouraged hijacking.
      They released political prisoners.

c They paid the ransom.
They need not have paid the ransom.

They kept their promise.
They allowed the hijacker to escape.
They accepted his demands.
They paid the passengers compensation.
They admitted that airport security was inadequate.

4 A My plane was hijacked. I sat and waited.
B *I would have tackled the hijacker.*

Tell **A** what *you would have done* in the following situations:
My house was on fire. I stood and watched.
A thief broke into my house. I hid under the bed.
My new TV broke so I threw it away.
I got lost so I sat down and cried.
I had a traffic accident and drove away without stopping.

5 We may express gratitude as follows:

Thanks for . . . (your help/helping me)
I'm very grateful to you for . . . (your help/helping me)
I appreciate your . . . (help, cooperation, etc.)

We may reply with:

Don't mention it.
That's O.K.
You're welcome.

Express gratitude to someone who:

helped you
lent you money
gave you advice
found a hotel room for you

Give suitable replies.

6 We hope he will be punished.
We are anxious that he be punished.

We hope the money will be returned.
We hope hijacking will be discouraged.
We hope security checks will be tightened up.
We hope there will be no more hijacking incidents.

7 Concorde

London to New York	Concorde	747
Price	£1226	£624
Flight time	3hrs 55min	7hrs 35min
No. of passengers	100	404–450
Fuel consumption	75 tons	10 tons

Part 1

Concorde is the fastest commercial aircraft in the world. It can fly at twice the speed of sound. It was developed jointly by Britain and France at a total cost of about £1500 million. When it first went into service with British Airways and Air France in 1969, it was hailed as a splendid technological achievement and large orders were anticipated from foreign airlines.

In order to recover the huge development costs, the governments of Britain and France needed to sell at least 150 Concordes to foreign airlines. No orders were received, however, and only 16 of the planes were ever built. The manufacturing plant was closed down in 1979.

At present, Concorde flies regularly from London and Paris to New York and Washington. Until recently, operating losses were so high that both British Airways and Air France were considering phasing out Concorde completely. Now, however, British Airways manages to make a small profit on its Concorde flights.

Reading comprehension

1 What is the maximum speed of Concorde?
2 How much did it cost to develop?
3 When was its first commercial flight?
4 How did people react to it initially?
5 Were the development costs recovered? Why (not)?
6 How many Concordes were built?
7 Are Concordes still being manufactured?
8 What routes is Concorde used on?
9 Why might it be phased out?

Discussion

Would you like to fly on Concorde? Why (not)?
Do you think such high speeds are necessary? Why (not)?
What kind of people use Concorde, do you think?

Vocabulary
Choose the words or phrases most similar in meaning to the
following as used in the reading passage:

commercial (a) business (b) private (c) operated for profit
jointly (a) together (b) partly (c) at the same time
hailed (a) acclaimed (b) called (c) recognized
anticipated (a) expected (b) promised (c) hoped for
recover (a) pay for (b) pay again (c) get back
phasing out (a) abolishing (b) closing down (c) gradually ending
    operation of

Part 2
Read through the following key words and phrases before listening
to the recording of an interview with a representative of British
Airways:

operational costs   fuel   oil crisis   decline
refuse landing permission   object to   sonic boom   envious
technological superiority

Listening comprehension
1 What does she think of Concorde?
2 Why haven't any foreign airlines bought it?
3 Why is it used on so few routes?
4 Why do some countries refuse to allow Concorde to use their
   airspace?
5 Will Concorde flights soon be abolished?

Role-play
Working in pairs, make up and act out a similar interview using the
above questions as a guide.

Part 3

> Letters to the Editor   New York Guardian
>
> Sir:
>
>   The decision of the city government to allow Concorde to land in New York is inexcusable. The noise it makes when taking off exceeds a hundred and twenty decibels, which is not only extremely painful but also dangerous to the health of people living near the airport. It has been proved to cause headaches, nausea, loss of appetite and depression and even, in some cases, nervous breakdowns. Concorde must not be allowed to land in New York.
>
>   Mary Dupree

Guided writing

Study the above letter and then write a similar letter explaining why the decision made by the city government was the right one. Use the outline below as a guide.

Sir,
   The decision . . . was the right one. Concorde is not only . . . but also . . . Furthermore, . . . People who live here must accept the decision of the city government or leave.

Discussion

Should Concorde be allowed to land in New York? Why (not)?

Part 4

Role-playing discussion

You are members of Tokyo's city government who have met to discuss whether or not Concorde should be allowed to fly regularly into Tokyo. Some of you support the idea; others are opposed to it. Each group must try to persuade the city governor to support their view. Use the arguments below and include others of your own.

For	Against
Tokyo to London – 18 hours by jumbo jet, only 6 hours by Concorde	Tokyo Airport is too small Concorde is too noisy Japan Airlines would lose customers
Japan is a progressive nation Relations with Britain and France are very important Tokyo is already very noisy	Concorde wastes precious fuel resources Concorde would pollute the air and damage the ozone layer

Part 5

Language practice

1 Notice how we ask people their opinions.
  What do you think of Concorde?

  Ask other students their opinion about:

  a TV program   a famous person (actor, singer, politician, etc.)
  a city (known to each student)   a controversial topic

2 We may present successive arguments or reasons using:
  For one thing, . . . For another . . .

  I like summer. For one thing, it seldom rains. For another, we can have long holidays.

  Present successive arguments for the following statements:

  Cars are very useful.
  I never smoke cigarettes.
  Television is a wonderful invention.
  Supersonic aircraft should not be built.
  Living in the country is very inconvenient.
  People should not drop litter.

3 Non-defining adjectival clauses usually begin with *who*, *whose* and *which*.

  We interviewed Phillipa Ashton, *who* is a representative of British Airways.
  We interviewed Phillipa Ashton, *whose* company operates Concorde.
  I flew on Concorde, *which* is the fastest commercial aircraft in the world.

Notice the difference between defining and non-defining clauses.

We are waiting for the plane which will arrive at 2 p.m. (*one of many planes* which will arrive today).

We are waiting for the plane, which will arrive at 2 p.m. (*only one plane* is expected today)

Combine the following sentences, changing the second sentence of each pair to a non-defining clause.

We interviewed Ms. Ashton. Her company operates Concorde.
We interviewed Ms. Ashton, whose company operates Concorde.

We ate at 'The Ginza'. It is a Japanese restaurant.
I spoke to Professor Stein. He is a famous economist.
He climbed Mount Everest. It is the highest mountain in the world.
She interviewed Paul Potter. His book is a best-seller.
I saw the 'Mona Lisa'. Da Vinci painted it.
I met Lord Ashford. I have wanted to meet him for a long time.

4 Combine the following sentences as shown in the example.

Operating losses are very high. As a result, they are considering phasing out Concorde.
Operating losses are so high that they are considering phasing out Concorde.

Concorde is very fast. It can cross the Atlantic in two hours.
Concorde is very noisy. As a result, people living near the airport suffer from severe headaches.
Development costs were very high. Therefore, taxes had to be raised.
Many foreign governments are jealous. Thus they refuse to allow Concorde to use their airspace.
Concorde is very big. Few airports can handle it.

8 Mysteries of the past

Part 1

Stonehenge is an ancient monument situated about ten miles north
of Salisbury in England. It was built about 4500 years ago, but by
whom and for what purpose remains a mystery. It consists of
concentric circles of large stones and holes. The builders must have
had a knowledge of geometry because the circles are symmetrical.
They may have been influenced by the Mycenaeans, whose
architecture was similar. Some of the stones, known as bluestones,
must have been brought from West Wales, over 135 miles away,
since that is the nearest place where such stones occur naturally.
Others, known as sarsen stones, must have come from
Marlborough, 18 miles away. These stones cannot have been
carried, since they are too heavy – some of them weigh more than
fifty tons. They must have been brought on rafts and rollers. Experts
say that it must have taken 1500 men more than five years to
transport the sarsen stones.

Stonehenge was probably built in three stages. First, settlers from
continental Europe built a temple for sun worship. Later, the
"Beaker" people added the stone circles. Finally, people of the
Wessex Culture settled in the area and transformed Stonehenge into
an observatory. By viewing the rising and setting of the sun and
moon through specific trilithons, they could calculate the exact time
of Midsummer and Midwinter and of the equinoxes. By moving
chalk balls around the fifty six holes which surround the monument,
they might even have been able to predict solar and lunar eclipses
and other astronomical events.

Although archaeologists have found out much about the origins of
Stonehenge, the biggest mystery remains unsolved. How did the
primitive builders of Stonehenge acquire their advanced knowledge
of astronomy?

Reading comprehension

1 Where is Stonehenge?
2 What does the symmetry of the circles prove?
3 Where can we find buildings of a similar design?
4 Why is it assumed that the bluestones came from West Wales?
5 How were the sarsen stones transported?
6 What was the original function of Stonehenge?
7 How was it used by people of the Wessex Culture?
8 What information could be obtained by looking through the
   trilithons?
9 What was the purpose of the 56 holes?
10 What is the biggest mystery?

Role-play

In pairs, take the parts of a tourist and a guide at Stonehenge. Ask
and answer questions on the following:

    the date of construction
    the origin of the stones
    how they were transported
    how long this took
    who built Stonehenge
    how they knew about geometry
    the purpose of the trilithons and the holes
    how the builders learned about astronomy

Vocabulary

1 Explain the meanings of these words and phrases as used in the text:

concentric	symmetrical
rafts	continental Europe
trilithons	equinoxes
eclipses	astronomy

2 Choose the words most similar in meaning to the following as used in the reading passage:

ancient (a) old (b) past (c) ruined
situated (a) built (b) located (c) found
transport (a) carry (b) move (c) deliver
probably (a) perhaps (b) most likely (c) surely
added (a) counted (b) included (c) built
viewing (a) watching (b) looking at (c) seeing

Part 2

Read through the list of key words and phrases before listening to the recording.

The speakers are Professor Adams, who presents his theory, Professor Beck, who doubts the theory, and Professor Court, who is neutral.

ancient literature	myths	Alexandria
sages	technology	Syene
astronomy	tremendous imaginations	geometry
documents	sphere	knowledge
Emperor Shun	rotate	source
Wright Brothers	Eratosthenes	Tibet
Sanskrit	calculate	Mesopotamia
detailed descriptions	diameter	disappear
manned flights	accurately	trace

Listening comprehension

1 What evidence is there to suggest that flying machines existed long ago?
2 Who was Eratosthenes and what did he do?
3 What is Professor Adams' theory of the source of all ancient knowledge?

Part 3

Guided writing

Study the description of Stonehenge carefully and then write a
similar description of an ancient monument (e.g. tomb, castle, etc.)
in your country or elsewhere.

Discussion

1 What do you think of the following theories?
   a Intelligent beings from Outer Space visited the earth thousands
     of years ago and taught the priests and sages of ancient
     civilizations.
   b A great civilization existed over 5000 years ago of which we
     know nothing and which disappeared without a trace.

2 What is your interpretation of this 3000-year-old rock carving
  located in Uzbekistan in the Soviet Union?

Quiz

1 Who first used the mathematical concept of zero?
   a the Romans b the Indian Brahmins c the Chinese

2 Who discovered America first?
   a the Vikings b Columbus c the Persians

3 When were electric batteries first used?
   a 200 years ago b 2000 years ago c 4000 years ago

4 Whose calculation of the age of the earth corresponds most closely
   to modern estimates?
   a the Greeks b the Egyptians c the Indian Brahmins

5 Who discovered penicillin first?
   a Fleming in 1928 b the Egyptians in 2000 B.C. c the Chinese in
   3000 B.C.

(Answers on page 113).

Part 4

Role-playing discussion

Workmen digging the foundations for a new apartment complex
have discovered the site of an ancient tomb which may be 5000 years
old. The city government must decide whether or not to allow the
apartments to be built.

In groups, take the parts of members of the city government (who
are divided in their opinion), the President of the construction
company and the Chairman of the local history society.

Factors of significance include:

   a serious housing shortage
   the possibility that the tomb contains vital information about an
   ancient civilization.

Part 5

Language practice

1 Answer these questions, using *must have*.

   What was Stonehenge used for?
   It must have been used for sun worship.

   Who was Stonehenge built by?
   Where were the sarsen stones brought from?
   How were the stones transported?

How long did it take to transport all the sarsen stones?
How did they calculate the exact time of Midsummer?

2 Answer these questions using *may have*.

Who were the builders of Stonehenge influenced by?
They may have been influenced by the Mycenaeans.

How many stages was Stonehenge built in?
What were the fifty-six holes used for?
Where was the original civilization located?
What happened to it?
How did the priests and sages of the original civilization get their knowledge?

3 Repeat exercise 2 using *might have* instead of *may have*.

4 Refute these statements, using *can't have*.

The ancient Chinese built flying machines.
They can't have built flying machines.

The sarsen stones were carried.
Columbus had a map of America when he started his journey.
The Babylonians knew about electricity.
Atlantis was located in Antarctica.
The Egyptian pyramids were built by spacemen.

5 Make deductions based on the following statements, using the cues.

The Chinese described flying machines. (tremendous imaginations)
They must have had tremendous imaginations.

The Babylonians knew about the moons of Jupiter. (telescopes)
Many Egyptian mummies have artificial teeth and bridges. (good dentists)
Columbus knew the shape of America. (maps)
Eratosthenes calculated the earth's diameter. (a good knowledge of geometry)
The library at Alexandria was the largest in the world. (a lot of books)

9 Prophets and prediction

A sixteenth-century French woodcut.

Part 1

In the sixteenth century, a remarkable French visionary named
Nostradamus wrote 600 predictions about the future. Since his
prophecies did not conform to the orthodox beliefs of the time, he
was obliged to write them in code in order to avoid being burned for
heresy.

In the twentieth century, many efforts have been made to interpret
the 600 quatrains in which the predictions of Nostradamus were
encoded. In 1938, a French scholar named de Fontbrune published
a book which attempted to explain some of the mysterious quatrains.
In his book, the German invasion of France and subsequent defeat
in 1945 were predicted, along with the exact date of Hitler's death.

However, de Fontbrune's interpretation did not receive widespread
acclaim until his son Jean-Charles, after seventeen years of research,
persuaded scientists at the National Research Council to put the
works of Nostradamus through a computer. The results were
published in a book entitled *Nostradamus, Historian and Prophet*, in
which an attempted assassination of the Pope in the year of an
electoral victory by the French Socialist Party was predicted. In
1981 both events occurred and the book became a best-seller.

According to de Fontbrune, the period from 1980 to 1999 will be
one of terrible upheaval during which Christianity will be defeated
by Islam and much of Western Europe, including Britain, will be
occupied by Russian soldiers. Finally, in the year 1999, there will be
a nuclear holocaust.

Reading comprehension

1 Who was Nostradamus and what did he do?
2 Why were his predictions written in code?
3 What events did de Fontbrune predict in 1938?
4 Did these predictions come true?
5 How did his son decode the writings of Nostradamus?
6 Why did his book become a best-seller?
7 What is predicted for the remaining years of this century?

Discussion

Can you believe the predictions of Nostradamus? Why (not)?
If so, how can these disasters be avoided?
What do you think will happen in the year 2000?

Vocabulary

Choose the words or phrases most similar in meaning to the
following as used in the reading passage:

remarkable (a) wonderful (b) noticeable (c) extraordinary
orthodox (a) popular (b) conventional (c) regulated
attempted (a) tried (b) succeeded (c) managed
subsequent (a) final (b) later (c) earlier
upheaval (a) movement (b) violent change (c) confusion

Part 2

Read through the following key words and phrases before listening
to the recording of an interview with Dr. Ramamurti, a famous
astrologer:

take place	accuracy
predetermined	heavenly bodies
observe	anticipate
optimistic	apocalypse
on the contrary	statesman
climate	

Listening comprehension

1 Why is Dr. Ramamurti famous?
2 How does she make accurate predictions?
3 When does she think the world will end?
4 Why does she reject current interpretations of the works of
   Nostradamus?
5 What major events has she predicted over the next ten years?
6 How can people find out more about those events?

Role-play

In pairs, take the parts of Dr. Ramamurti and an interviewer. Ask
and answer questions on:

   how she foretells the future
   if she thinks the world will end in 1999
   what she thinks of current interpretations of Nostradamus
   what events she has predicted in the next few years

Discussion

Do you believe in astrology? In what other ways might the future be
predicted?
Do you believe that all events are predetermined?
Would you like to know the future? Why (not)?
What do you think of the predictions of Dr. Ramamurti?
Which statesman and countries do you think might be involved?
If you could ask Dr. Ramamurti one question about the future, what
would you ask? What answer might you be given?

Part 3

Discussion

Which of the following dangers do you fear most?

traffic accidents	unemployment
fire	disease
war	violent crime
pollution	food shortage
burglary	fascism
water shortage	earthquakes
inflation	

Rank them according to degree of (a) fearfulness (b) avoidability
Which are caused by man and which by nature?
What can you do to avoid or escape from these dangers?

Guided writing

Find a report in an English newspaper about an accident or incident
involving one of the above dangers. List the key points and then
rewrite the report in your own words without looking at the original.

Part 4

Role-playing discussion

An astrologer whose predictions have never been wrong has
predicted that your city will be struck by a major earthquake within
one year. The area has never experienced tremors before. You, the
city government, must decide what, if anything, to do. The
following ideas might be considered:

   prepare an emergency evacuation plan
   reinforce structurally-weak public buildings (e.g. schools)
   advise citizens to prepare emergency survival kits (specify the
   contents)

establish a research center to monitor minute tremors and changes
in underground water pressures and temperatures which could
indicate an impending earthquake
do nothing and hope the astrologer was wrong

Part 5

Language practice

Transform the following sentences as shown in the examples.

1 If he hadn't written them in code, he would have been burned.
He wrote them in code in order to avoid being burned.

If she hadn't jumped back, she would have been hit by the car.
If the pilot hadn't obeyed the hijacker, he would have been killed.
If the bank robbers hadn't worn masks, they would have been
recognized.
If the children hadn't lied to their parents, they would have been
punished.
If I hadn't studied hard, I would have failed the exam.

2 They say you predicted certain events.
You are said to have predicted certain events.

They know you have learned a lot about the stars.
They believe your predictions were accurate.
They say you have written a new book.
They assume you have rejected the predictions of Nostradamus.

3 When the interviewer asks Dr. Ramamurti about his method of
prediction, he says:
if you don't mind my asking . . .

We often use this expression when asking personal or
embarrassing questions.

We may refuse to answer as follows:
I'd rather not answer/go into that.
I'm afraid I can't answer.
(N.B. Silence may be interpreted as hostility.)

Using the above expressions, try to find out the following
information from another student

how much his/her parents earn
how old he/she is
if he/she has ever been drunk
if he/she has ever broken the law
if he/she believes in God

10 Our environment

Part 1

Scientists have recently reported that the polar ice caps are melting, due to a rise in atmospheric temperatures known as the "Greenhouse Effect". According to Melvin Calvin, who won a Nobel Prize for earlier research, the carbon dioxide given off when coal and oil are burned is accumulating in the atmosphere and causing temperatures to rise. As a result, the ice covering the North and South Poles is melting and may eventually lead to a rise in sea levels which could flood many areas of the world, including New York, London and Tokyo.

The "Greenhouse Effect" is just one of many fundamental changes which are taking place in the environment. Tropical rain forests which took fifty million years to grow are being reduced at the rate of fourteen acres per minute. The world's deserts are growing year by year. Scandinavia's beautiful lakes are becoming lifeless due to "acid rain" caused by sulphur dioxide emissions from factories in West Germany and Britain. Many species of animals and plants are threatened with extinction.

In presenting the results of "Global 2000", the U.S. Government's most comprehensive study of the future, Edmund Muskie said, "World population growth, the degradation of the Earth's natural resource base and the spread of environmental pollution collectively threaten the welfare of mankind." Words alone, however, will not solve the problem. If governments do not act quickly and decisively to protect the environment, this planet will soon become uninhabitable.

Reading comprehension

1 What is the "Greenhouse Effect"?
2 What causes it?
3 What serious effects may it eventually have?
4 What is happening to the world's deserts?
5 How fast are tropical forests shrinking?
6 What causes acid rain?
7 How is it affecting lakes in Scandinavia?
8 What may happen to many animals and plants?
9 What was "Global 2000"?
10 What are the three main factors which endanger the welfare of mankind, according to Edmund Muskie?
11 What will happen if the environment is not protected?

Discussion

What environmental problems exist in your country?
What should be done about them?
Why are many governments slow to take the necessary measures?

Vocabulary

Choose the word or phrase most similar in meaning to the following as used in the reading passage:

melting (a) evaporating (b) becoming warmer (c) becoming liquid
accumulating (a) increasing (b) staying (c) spreading
eventually (a) finally (b) later (c) soon
fundamental (a) basic (b) important (c) serious
threatened with (a) warned of (b) promised (c) in danger of
extinction (a) death (b) disaster (c) extermination of species
comprehensive (a) understandable (b) detailed (c) including many
    things
uninhabitable (a) extinct (b) impossible to live on (c) deserted

Part 2

Read through the list of key words and phrases before listening to the recording of an interview with Professor O'Sullivan, a well-known ecologist.

environmental crisis	self-generating capability
oxygen	bring about
drastic	mass production
Industrial Revolution	significant
avert	ecological recovery

Listening comprehension

1 What has happened to our major ecosystems?
2 How will this affect the human race?
3 What are the main causes of this crisis?
4 What should be done to protect the environment?
5 How long would it take for the ecology to recover completely?

Role-play

Working in pairs, act out this dialogue, using the above questions as a guide.

Part 3

The average city with 500,000 inhabitants produces over 500 tons of garbage per day. This is usually burned, causing air pollution, or dumped on wasteland, becoming an eyesore. Until recently, little effort has been made to recycle the waste.

"Stardust 80" is a garbage disposal facility which was built on reclaimed land in Yokohama. It employs a new system of waste treatment which was developed by the Japanese Government Agency of Industrial Science and Technology. It can handle 100 tons of garbage in eight hours.

It consists of a pre-processing plant and sub-plants. The pre-processing plant sorts garbage into metal, plastics, paper and kitchen refuse. It is eight metres long and three metres wide. The sorted garbage is then treated by the sub-plants, which convert plastics into fuel gas, paper into pulp and kitchen refuse into compost. Metals are recovered as scrap.

"Stardust 80" cost about 20 million dollars to build. It is somewhat more expensive than a similar-sized incineration plant but much of the cost may be recovered in the long run through the sale of recycled materials.

Role-play

You are the representative of a city government which is considering buying a "Stardust"-type plant. Interview the director of the plant to find out:

   the location of the plant
   its capacity
   who the system was developed by
   what the plant consists of
   what it does
   the size of the pre-processing plant
   the cost of the plant
   its long-term advantages

Guided writing

Prepare sales literature for the "Moondust 85" garbage disposal facility. Within 150 words, say what it does, including all the data shown below and emphasizing its advantages over other methods of treating garbage.

capacity: 1200 tons of garbage per day
size: pre-processing plant 150 cubic metres
      sub plants 120–150 cubic metres each
pollution: nil
cost: 50 million dollars
approximate period needed for delivery and installment: 10 months

recovered materials for a typical city (*per 100 tons of garbage*):

compost: 28 tons
paper pulp: 25 tons
scrap metal: 3 tons
fuel gas 7500 cubic metres

Part 4

Role-playing discussion

The government of a European city with a population of 400,000 people is considering two proposals for the purchase of garbage treatment facilities. The first proposal is to buy a locally-made incineration plant costing 10 million pounds, capable of treating 250 tons of garbage per day. The second proposal is to buy a Japanese-made plant similar to "Stardust 80" costing 18 million pounds, capable of treating 180 tons of garbage per day.

In groups, take the following roles:

a representative of the local company which would make the incineration plant
a representative of the Japanese company
two city-council members in favor of the first proposal
two city-council members in favor of the second proposal
one city-council member in favor of neither proposal

Each participant must try to convince the city-council member who is in favor of neither proposal to support one of the two proposals.

Part 5

Language practice

Combine these sentences as shown in the example.

1 Melvin Calvin says carbon dioxide is accumulating.
   He won a Nobel Prize.
   Melvin Calvin, who won a Nobel Prize, says carbon dioxide is accumulating.

   Edwin Muskie presented the report. He was a senator.
   My brother is worried about the environment. He is a scientist.
   The President could take the necessary action. He has a lot of power.
   Industrialists do not care about pollution. They are concerned about profits.

Prince Philip believes endangered species must be protected. He is President of the World Wildlife Fund.

2 Sea levels are rising. This could flood many areas.
   Sea levels are rising, which could flood many areas.

   Trees are being cut down. This leads to soil erosion.
   Coal is burned. This gives off carbon dioxide.
   The environment is being degraded. This threatens our lives.
   Deserts are growing. This causes food shortages.
   Scientists are worried. This shows that the problem is serious.

3 Even if pollution were controlled strictly, the ecosystem would never recover.
   Even with strict control of pollution, the ecosystem would never recover.

   Even if birth control were practised universally, the population would continue to grow.
   Even if new forests were planted extensively, it would take years to restore the ecological balance.
   Even if endangered species were protected legally, many of them would soon become extinct.
   Even if garbage were recycled efficiently, scarce resources would still be wasted in other ways.
   Even if new facilities were constructed immediately, some garbage would still need to be burned.

4 In the recorded interview, Professor O'Sullivan answers a question as follows:

   Interviewer: Can anything be done . . . ?
   Professor O'Sullivan: I doubt it.

   This answer indicates uncertainty with a negative expectation. The following answers indicate uncertainty with a positive expectation.

   I imagine so.
   I expect so.
   I think so.
   Probably (not).

   Answer the following questions with one of the above answers.

   Will many species become extinct?
   Will the ecology recover quickly?
   Will the world's population continue to grow?
   Will the human race survive?
   Will man become extinct?

11 Smoking

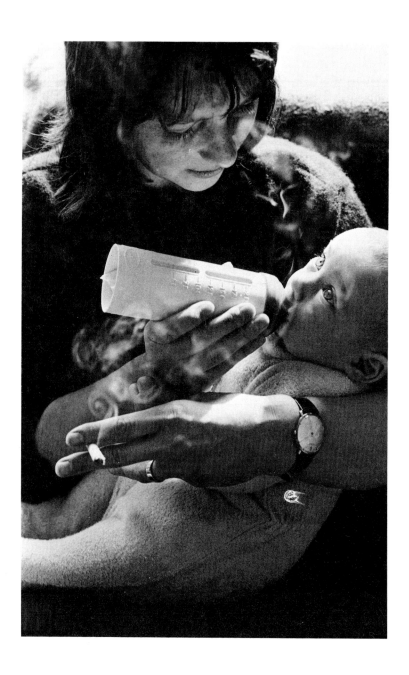

Number of smokers expressed as % of adult population		
Country	Male	Female
Australia	40	31
Austria	33	22
Canada	38.6	30.1
Denmark	60.7	45.9
Finland	36	19
France	50	26
W. Germany	41	28
Japan	73.1	15.4
New Zealand	38	31
Norway	43	33
Sweden	26	26
U.K.	38	33
U.S.A.	36.7	28.9

Part 1

A report on smoking published in 1979 by the U.S. Surgeon General shows that over fifty million Americans, including six million teenagers, smoke cigarettes regularly, and that 346,000 Americans died the previous year of diseases related to heavy smoking. Research conducted in many countries has indicated that smoking causes lung cancer, heart disease and various respiratory ailments and that pregnant women who smoke run the risk of having deformed babies.

Responding to overwhelming medical evidence of the harmful effects of smoking, many governments have taken action to reduce tobacco consumption. Some have imposed heavy taxes on tobacco products; others have prohibited cigarette commercials and conducted anti-smoking campaigns. None, however, has even considered prohibiting the sale of tobacco. This is due partly to the political power of the big tobacco companies and partly to the fact that so many people, particularly in influential positions in society, are habitual smokers. Tobacco farmers and workers are also strongly opposed to legislation.

Reading comprehension

1 According to researchers, what illnesses are caused by heavy smoking?
2 How many Americans died of such diseases in 1978?
3 What might happen if a woman smokes regularly during pregnancy?
4 In what ways have various governments tried to reduce tobacco consumption?
5 Is the sale of tobacco prohibited in any country? Why (not)?

Vocabulary

Choose the words most similar in meaning to the following as used in the reading passage:

indicated (a) shown (b) proven (c) suggested
ailments (a) illnesses (b) difficulties (c) injuries
deformed (a) sick (b) retarded (c) misshapen
overwhelming (a) convincing (b) strong (c) irresistible
prohibited (a) forbidden (b) restricted (c) discouraged
particularly (a) only (b) mainly (c) especially

Role-play

Interview the U.S. surgeon general to find out:

the number of teenage smokers
the number of Americans who died of diseases related to heavy smoking in 1978
the harmful effects of heavy smoking
the risks of smoking for pregnant women
the measures which the Government could take to reduce tobacco consumption
the reasons why the sale of tobacco has not been prohibited
if he smokes himself

Survey

1 Interview other students to find out whether they smoke or not.

2 Ask the smokers these questions:

How long have you been smoking?
Why did you take up smoking?
How many cigarettes do you smoke per day?
Do you worry about the harmful effects on your health?

Have you ever tried to give up smoking?
Do you think the sale of tobacco should be restricted? Why (not)?

3 Ask the non-smokers these questions:

Why don't you smoke?
What do you think of people who smoke?
Do you think the sale of tobacco should be restricted or
prohibited? Why (not)?

Part 2

Listen to the recording of a conversation between a husband and
wife.

Listening comprehension

1 Why does John smoke?
2 What is his wife worried about?
3 What happened the last time he tried to quit smoking?
4 What does his wife suggest he do this time?
5 Does he think it would be successful?
6 What does he promise to do?

Role-play

Make up a similar dialogue based on the following outline.

Your friend tries to discourage you from smoking, giving his
reasons.
You explain why you smoke.
Your friend suggests that you should give it up, explaining that it is
bad for his health too.
You remind him of how irritable you were last time you tried.
He suggests you cut down gradually.
You promise to try.

The following expressions may be useful:

I wish you wouldn't . . .
I think you should . . .
Why don't you . . .
All right, I'll try . . .

Part 3

To the Editor.

Sir:

I wish to draw the attention of smokers to the suffering which they thoughtlessly inflict on other people. It has been proven beyond doubt that when a person smokes, he subjects the people around him not only to great discomfort but also to physical harm. Yet offices, shops, restaurants and even hospital waiting rooms are filled with clouds of tobacco smoke. Since smokers are evidently too selfish to refrain voluntarily from smoking in public places, they must be required to do so by law.

Lesley Hart

1 What is the writer of this letter complaining about?
2 What does she think should be done? Why?

Discussion

Should smoking in public places be prohibited or restricted? Why (not)? If so, in which places? What kind of penalties should be imposed?

Guided writing

Study the above letter carefully and then write a similar letter complaining about car exhaust and advocating the banning of cars from downtown areas.

Part 4

Role-playing discussion

You are members of a legislative commission set up to consider anti-smoking legislation. Discuss the following proposals and any others you may have and try to reach a consensus on which proposals to recommend for legislation.

1 Prohibition of smoking in all public buildings.
2 Prohibition of smoking in specific public buildings (e.g. hospitals)
3 All public buildings to provide separate facilities for smokers and non-smokers.

4 Prohibition of smoking on all buses, trains and planes.
5 All buses, trains and planes to have separate sections for smokers and non-smokers.

Part 5

Language practice

1 Combine the following sentences as shown in the example.

A report was published in 1979.
It shows that fifty million Americans smoke.
A report published in 1979 shows that fifty million Americans smoke.

Research was conducted in many countries.
It indicates that smoking is harmful.

Action has been taken by many governments.
It has failed to reduce tobacco consumption.

People have been warned of the risks of smoking.
They seldom pay any attention.

A new law was passed a few years ago.
It required warnings to be printed on cigarette packages.

2 When we object to other people's bad habits, we may use the following expressions:

I wish you wouldn't . . .
You really shouldn't . . .
Do you mind not . . . ing . . . ?

Use these expressions to object to the following habits:

using bad language   borrowing your things without asking
littering   driving dangerously
slamming doors   playing the trumpet late at night

3 When we want to encourage people to do something, we may use the following expressions:

I think you should . . .
Don't you think you should . . . ?

Use these expressions to give appropriate advice to someone who:

drives dangerously   beats his wife
drinks too much   is rude to everyone
always fails exams   has been unemployed for a long time

12 The welfare state

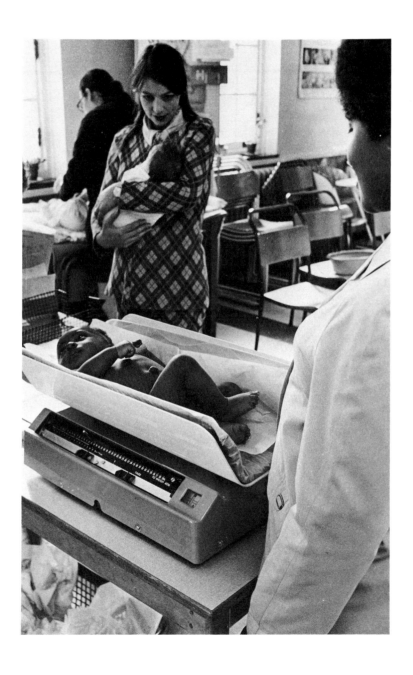

Part 1

Britain spends about 15% of its Gross National Product on welfare, less than other European countries such as Sweden and the Netherlands, but sufficient to ensure that none of its citizens die of starvation.

In return for weekly contributions made during periods of regular employment, the National Insurance scheme provides weekly cash benefits during periods of sickness and unemployment and after retirement.

Sickness benefits are paid for an unlimited period but unemployment benefits are only payable for periods of unemployment of up to one year. The social security system provides a subsistence income for people who are not entitled to receive unemployment benefits.

Weekly pensions are payable to those who retire at the minimum pension age (65 for a man and 60 for a woman) and to those who continue to work for more than five years after the minimum pension age.

In addition to sickness and unemployment benefits and pensions, all British citizens are entitled to receive free medical treatment under the National Health Service.

A generous welfare state must be financed by high taxes. In Britain, taxation amounts to 37% of the national income. Most British taxpayers agree, however, that paying high taxes is preferable to letting fellow citizens starve.

Reading comprehension

1 How much does Britain spend on welfare?
2 Who is entitled to receive cash benefits under the National Insurance scheme?
3 For how long are such benefits payable?
4 How can people who are unemployed for more than a year subsist?
5 Who is entitled to receive a pension?
6 What does the National Health Service provide?
7 How is the British welfare state financed?
8 How do taxpayers feel about this?

Discussion

Compare the British welfare state with that of your own country.
Would you prefer to have a generous welfare state with a high level
of taxation or a frugal welfare state with a low level of taxation?
Why?

Vocabulary

Choose the words or phrases most similar in meaning to the
following as used in the reading passage:

sufficient (a) plenty (b) enough (c) much
ensure (a) prove (b) ascertain (c) make sure
up to (a) at least (b) at the most (c) during
generous (a) kind (b) costly (c) sympathetic
are entitled to (a) should (b) may (c) must

Guided writing

Write a similar description of the welfare system of your own
country.

Part 2

Read through the following key words and phrases before listening
to the recording of an interview with a well-known member of
parliament, Mary Lloyd:

    parasites
    laid off
    declining industries
    industrial retraining schemes

Listening comprehension

1 Why does Mrs. Lloyd think the present welfare system should be
   changed?
2 What changes has she proposed?
3 What effects does she think these changes would have?

Role-play

Act out this interview using the above questions as a guide.

Part 3

Investigations have shown that many unemployed workers are reluctant to seek jobs even though many vacancies remain unfilled. For example, in February 1979 London had 146,000 unemployed workers and 150,000 job vacancies.

The following interview with a man who has just collected his weekly unemployment benefit may help to explain this situation.

Reporter Excuse me. I'm writing a report on unemployment. I wonder if I might ask you a few questions?

Man By all means. What would you like to know?

Reporter How long have you been on welfare?

Man For ten months.

Reporter Where did you use to work?

Man In a car factory.

Reporter How did you become unemployed?

Man I was laid off because of the recession.

Reporter Have you tried to find a job?

Man Yes, of course. But I haven't had any luck.

Reporter But surely there are many vacancies, aren't there?

Man Yes, but they're all for unskilled labor. I've been designing cars for twenty years. Why should I wash dishes or sweep streets for the same amount of money as I'm getting on welfare?

Reporter Do you intend to go on collecting unemployment benefit until you find a suitable job?

Man Yes. Why not? I've paid taxes for twenty years. I've got a right to receive something in return, haven't I?

Reporter Yes, I suppose you have. Well thank you very much for this interview.

Man Don't mention it.

Role-play

1 Working in pairs, act out this dialogue.
2 Make up similar dialogues with:
    a an unemployed teacher who lost her job six months ago when the Government cut education expenses and has since been offered low-paid jobs in shops and restaurants
    b an unemployed English major who has been looking for a suitable job for two years and has only been offered low-paid jobs in bakeries and laundries.

Discussion

What do you think of the attitude shown by the man in the interview?
What would you do if you were in his position? Why?

Part 4

Role-playing discussion

In groups, take the parts of four politicians who are discussing Mrs. Lloyd's proposals.

The politicians are:

  a Conservative concerned about high taxes
  a Socialist concerned about high unemployment
  a Liberal concerned about the shortage of skilled labor in growing industries
  an Independent anxious to keep his seat in the next election

Part 5

Language practice

Transform the following sentences as shown in the example.

1 It is better to work than to starve.
   Working is preferable to starving.

   It is better to pay high taxes than to let fellow citizens starve.
   It is better to get a low-paid job than to live on welfare.
   It is better to subsist on social security than to beg in the streets.
   It is better to teach workers new skills than to pay them for doing nothing.
   It is better to take a low-paying job at once than to wait a long time for a highly-paid job.

2 I propose a reduction in unemployment benefit.
   I propose that unemployment benefit be reduced.

   I propose an expansion in retraining schemes.
   I propose an increase in pensions.
   I propose some changes in the welfare system.
   I propose an improvement in working conditions.
   I propose a cut in taxes.

3 When asking permission formally, we often say:
   I wonder if I might . . . ?
   I wonder if I could . . . ?

Suitable answers are:

By all means.   I'm sorry but . . .
Yes, of course.   I'd rather you didn't.

Practice these expressions with the following prompts:

. . . ask you a few questions
. . . use your telephone
. . . borrow your dictionary
. . . take one of these pamphlets
. . . speak to your father
. . . take a photograph of you

13 Marriage and divorce

Part 1

The traditional wedding vow to stay together "till death us do part" is becoming obsolete in most western countries as divorce rates continue to rise steadily. In the U.S., for example, the statistics for 1978 show one divorce for every two marriages; in that year, over a million couples had their marriages dissolved, often at high financial and social cost.

One factor behind the steady rise in divorce rates, according to sociologists, is the changing status of women. More and more women are continuing to work after marriage, thus remaining financially independent. Moreover, they are becoming less tolerant of husbands who treat them as subordinates. Another important factor is the gradual relaxation of divorce laws in many states. It is now relatively easy to obtain an uncontested divorce on the grounds of irretrievable breakdown of marriage.

While divorce is often the only satisfactory solution for married couples who can no longer stand the sight of each other, it can have a traumatic effect on their children. It is estimated that one in four American children currently lives with only one parent. Many such children grow up to be emotionally unstable and unable to cope with the pressures of modern society. They are the principal victims of divorce.

Reading comprehension

1 What is causing the traditional wedding vow to become obsolete?
2 How many people were divorced in the U.S. in 1978?
3 What two factors have caused divorce rates to rise?
4 Why is it difficult for unemployed married women to divorce their husbands?
5 What attitude shown by husbands makes many wives angry?
6 What reason might be given for a divorce desired by both husband and wife?
7 Who suffers the most from rising divorce rates?
8 How are they affected?

Discussion

Is divorce common in your country? Why (not)?
Under what circumstances do you think divorce should be permitted?
Should women continue to work after marriage? Why (not)?

Vocabulary

Choose the word or phrase most similar in meaning to the following as used in the reading passage:

vow (a) guarantee (b) contract (c) promise
obsolete (a) out-dated (b) old (c) useless
dissolved (a) liquefied (b) terminated (c) separated
moreover (a) however (b) furthermore (c) indeed
tolerant (a) patient (b) forgiving (c) obedient
subordinates (a) inferiors (b) servants (c) nonentities
uncontested (a) unrivalled (b) unchallenged (c) unopposed
stand (a) bear (b) allow (c) accept
traumatic (a) terrible (b) harmful (c) emotionally shocking
principal (a) main (b) first (c) most important

Part 2

Read through the following key words and phrases before listening to the recording of an interview with a marriage counsellor:

deep insight	disillusioned
roles	idealistic
concessions	give and take
sacrifice	tedious
soul-destroying	

Listening comprehension

1 How long has Mr. Thurber been a marriage counsellor?
2 What does he consider to be the most common problem of married couples?
3 What do they become disillusioned with? Why?
4 What kinds of concessions are necessary?
5 What often happens when married couples are unable to cope with their marital problems?
6 How can such marriages be saved?
7 Has Mr. Thurber been successful in marriage?

Role-play

Interview Mr. Thurber to find out:

> how long he has been a marriage counsellor
> the most common problem of married couples
> what he means by 'disillusioned'

what kinds of concessions are necessary
what couples should do when their marriage is in trouble
if he is married

Part 3

Announcement

On 17 July 1984, Henry and Wilma Foster will celebrate their
eightieth wedding anniversary. A reception in their honor is to be
held at the Mission Hall on Main Street from 6 p.m. All relatives
and acquaintances are invited to attend.

Role-play

In pairs (or threes), take the parts of a newspaper reporter, Henry
and/or Wilma. Ask and answer questions on the following:

where they first met
their first impressions of each other
what they did on their first date
their ages at that time
how long their courtship lasted
what their first quarrel was about
when Henry proposed to Wilma
what he said
what she replied
their parents' reactions
where the wedding took place
what the bride wore
where they spent their honeymoon
when their first child was born
how many children they had
how many grandchildren they have
if they have any great grandchildren
the secret of their successful marriage

Discussion

Are you married?
If so, how did you meet your partner? How did you spend your
honeymoon?

If not, in what order of importance would you rate the following factors in choosing a partner?

physical attractiveness	personal charm
intelligence	sense of humor
wealth	energy
strength of character	sincerity
any other factor	

Part 4

1 Describe a typical wedding ceremony or reception in your own country. Refer to the location, the participants and guests, the clothes worn by the bride and groom and the procedure.
2 Complete this application form for a computer date.
   Your answers need not be truthful!

Details of applicant: Details of preferred partner:

Name ....   Age ....

Address ....   Marital status ....

Age ....   Educational background ....

Marital status
    (single/married/divorced)   Desired traits ....

Occupation ....

Educational background ....   Objectionable traits ....

Hobbies ....

Favorite kind of (a) music   ....
                 (b) food
Personal strengths ....

Personal weaknesses ....

Part 5

Language practice

Transform the following sentences as shown in the examples.

1 Their marriage was dissolved.
   They had their marriage dissolved.

   His hair was cut.
   Our house was painted.
   Her photograph was taken.
   Their car was repaired.
   My eyes were tested.

2 Obtaining a divorce is easy.
   It is easy to obtain a divorce.

   Finding a suitable partner is difficult.
   Driving on the wrong side of the road is dangerous.
   Interrupting when someone is talking is bad manners.
   Paying women less than men for doing the same job is unfair.
   Finding a cheap apartment in New York is almost impossible.

3 Asking someone to be more explicit.
   This may be done in various ways.

   What exactly do you mean (by . . .)?
   Concessions? What kind of concessions?
   Disillusioned? In what way?

   Working in pairs, practise these techniques with the statements
   below:

   A It's necessary to make concessions.
   B *Concessions? What kind of concessions?*
   A For the husband, it may mean . . . (etc.)

   The traditional wedding vow is becoming obsolete.
   The cost of divorce is very high.
   Women are becoming less tolerant.
   Children are victims.
   They start off with fantasies.
   There is a great deal of stress.

14 The energy crisis

Odeillo, Pyrenees, France.

Part 1

Table 1 Production of oil 1978 (millions of tons)	
*OPEC	1500
U.S.S.R.	572
U.S.A.	488
China	96
Mexico	66
U.K.	53
Others	289
Total	3084

Table 2 User's sources of energy 1977 (%)	Oil	Others
U.S.A.	48	52
W. Germany	52	48
U.K.	34	66
France	60	40
Japan	77	23

*OPEC = Organization of Petroleum Exporting Countries (including Middle East, Venezuela, Nigeria and Indonesia)

Industrialized nations depend on fossil fuels (mainly oil, gas and coal) for most of their energy. Oil is the most popular source of energy, being easy to transport and, until recently, relatively cheap. It supplies about half of the energy needs of the U.S.A. and Western Europe. Although the Soviet Union is currently the world's biggest producer of oil, nearly 60% of the world's proven reserves lie in the Middle East, a politically volatile region. The dangers of depending primarily on the Middle East to supply a commodity of such importance to the prosperity of the western world became obvious in 1973, when a politically-motivated interruption in oil supplies by Arab producers led to an oil crisis which caused prices to rise sharply and threatened the economic stability of the world. As a result, the major non-communist oil-importing nations agreed at a series of summit meetings to make efforts to reduce their consumption of oil and to develop alternative sources of energy.

Reading comprehension

1 Why is oil the most popular source of energy?
2 Where are the world's largest oil reserves located?
3 Why is it risky to rely on the Middle East for oil supplies?
4 What was the cause of the oil crisis in 1973?
5 What effect did the oil crisis have?
6 What did oil-consuming nations do about this problem?

Vocabulary

Choose the word or phrase most similar in meaning to the following as used in the reading passage:

currently (a) now (b) presently (c) recently
proven (a) potential (b) confirmed (c) decided
volatile (a) inflammable (b) unstable (c) dangerous
commodity (a) good (b) material (c) fuel
make efforts (a) struggle (b) try (c) persevere
alternative (a) more convenient (b) other (c) better

Part 2

Read through the following key words and phrases before listening to the recording of an interview with Professor Watson, a famous economist:

prolonged international recession	sustain
consumption	output
generate	discover
mention	controversial
in addition to	radioactive leakage
satisfactory	storage
disposal	confess
hazards	disturbing
look forward to	nuclear fusion

Listening comprehension

1 According to some experts, what will happen to the world economy within a few years? Why?
2 Does Professor Watson agree with these predictions? Why (not)?
3 Why is nuclear energy a controversial subject?
4 How does Professor Watson feel about atomic power?

Role-play

Interview Professor Watson to find out:

her views on predictions that a fall in oil supply will lead to an international recession
her opinion of nuclear energy

Part 3

Government representatives and scientific experts from all over the world are attending an energy conference in London. This is the program for the morning of the first day:

2 July 19..

  9.30 Solar Energy   Professor Jean-Pierre Pascal
10.00 Geothermal Energy   Doctor Ivan Melenkov
10.30 Biological Energy   Professor Otto Halsborg
11.00 Conservation   Michael Williams
11.30 Energy   Doctor Francis Burns

These are the notes which the speakers will use:

Solar energy	Method – use sunshine to heat water or convert sunshine to electricity directly by using solar cells.
Advantages	cost-free, unlimited supplies, pollution-free, safe, little maintenance required.
Disadvantages	irregular supplies (depend on weather), high costs of solar cells for energy conversion.
Application	small-scale projects – especially in developing countries, e.g. for supplying power for irrigation pumps or for evaporating salt water to provide drinking water; also solar panels on roofs of public buildings to provide hot water, e.g. White House in Washington (system cost $28,000) large scale projects – solar power stations, e.g. Nio in Japan (generates 10,000 kilowatts)
Geothermal energy	Method – utilize hot springs and subterranean heat
Advantages	cost-free, unlimited supplies, pollution-free, safe, easily convertible.
Disadvantages	only available in certain areas, high cost of construction of power plant.
Application	for heating cities, also in geothermal power stations, e.g. Pauzhet in U.S.S.R., Yellowstone National Park in U.S.A. (Total world generating capacity 1.5 million kilowatts at present.)
Biological energy	Method – grow plants (e.g. milkweed) which contain oil.

Advantages	low-cost, oil plants may be grown on barren land, pollution-free, safe, easily convertible.
Disadvantages	requires large areas of land (over 70 million acres needed to supply 10% of energy needs of U.S.A.)
Application	for producing petroleum and other oil derivatives, also for use in thermal power stations, e.g. Alabama, U.S.A., a 26,000 acre milkweed plantation (-estimated yield 160 barrels of oil per acre at $15 per barrel)

Energy conservation	Method – eliminate energy waste, e.g. by redesigning buildings, machines and vehicles.
Advantages	safe, pollution-free
Disadvantages	high costs of new facilities and vehicles, public resistance to changes in lifestyles.
Proposals	increase taxes on oil for industrial use and gasoline for cars: restrict T.V. viewing hours, late-night entertainment (clubs, bars, etc.) and use of neon signs for advertising purposes; introduce energy-saving regulations for new buildings (both public and private), e.g. compulsory double-glazing and roof insulation.

Nuclear energy	Method – Fission (splitting) of atoms. Thus releasing great heat.
Advantages	large supplies of fissionable materials, large power output
Disadvantages	danger of radioactive leakage, problem of disposal of radio-active waste, high initial cost of construction of power plant, large amounts of water needed for cooling the atomic reactor, opposition from environmentalists
Application	in nuclear power plants, producing electricity in ships (e.g. icebreakers and submarines) or spacecraft, requiring energy for long periods of time
Statistics	In U.S.A., 74 nuclear power plants with total capacity of nearly 60 million kilowatts. Total world capacity nearly 150 million kilowatts.

Role-play

Using the notes shown on the previous page, students will give short lectures on one of the five topics.

Part 4

Role-playing discussion

You are members of the government's Economic Planning Committee which must decide on an energy policy for the next 10 years. Due to budgetary restraints it can only spend 10,000 million dollars on new projects. An estimated 100,000 kilowatts will be needed. The following projects have been proposed:

1 nuclear power plant costing 10,000 million dollars, capable of generating 250,000 kilowatts

2 geothermal power plants costing 5000 million dollars each, capable of generating 40,000 kilowatts each

8 solar power plants costing 1000 million dollars each, capable of generating 12,000 kilowatts each

2 conventional coal-burning power plants costing 4000 million dollars each, capable of generating 60,000 kilowatts each

energy conservation policies costing 10,000 million dollars, capable of saving 100,000 kilowatts

Each member will explain how the money should be spent and why. Attempt to reach a consensus. Important facts to consider are: safety, effects on the environment, the durability of the plant and fuel and maintenance costs.

Guided writing

Write a report presenting one of the five topics shown in note form.

Part 5

Language practice

Transform the sentences as shown in the examples.

1 The dangers became obvious in 1973. Oil supplies were interrupted then.
The dangers became obvious in 1973, when oil supplies were interrupted.

They stopped building Concordes in 1979. The manufacturing plant was closed down then.

Nostradamus wrote in the sixteenth century. The Catholic Church was very powerful then.
I gave up smoking last October. My uncle died of cancer then.
Most men retire at the age of 65. They are entitled to a pension then.
Nuclear power will be important in 1990. It will generate 13% of the world's electricity then.

2 I think it is very disturbing.
   I find it very disturbing.

   I thought the book was very interesting.
   Many people think nuclear power is frightening.
   I'm sure you will think this movie is very funny.
   He thinks his new job is rather boring.

3 They are discovering new sources of energy all the time.
   New sources of energy are being discovered all the time.

   They will solve the problem of radioactive leakage.
   They are going to construct a nuclear power plant.
   They have developed more efficient production methods.
   They must find new sources of energy.
   They are conducting research on nuclear fusion.

4 We may ask people's opinions in the following ways:
   What is your opinion of . . . ?
   What are your views on . . . ?
   What do you think of . . . ?
   How do you feel about . . . ?
   Now use these expressions to find out each other's opinions on the following issues:

nuclear energy	the advertising of harmful products
rent stabilization	Concorde
private education	the predictions of Nostradamus
hijacking	

   Continue, using your own ideas.

15 Crime and punishment

| Crime rates per 100,000 population 1980 | | | | | | |
City	murders	robberies	assaults	thefts	rapes	total
New York	20.1	989.4	578.3	5983.3	51.9	7623.0
Chicago	25.4	491.5	333.2	5263.9	43.3	5965.9
Los Angeles	23.9	627.2	607.8	7207.4	90.3	8556.8
London	4.2	93.8	196.7	6254.0	6.4	6555.1
Paris	6.8	479.1	168.4	8079.1	6.8	8739.2
W. Berlin	6.4	119.3	234.3	6837.6	26.2	7223.8
Hamburg	4.7	91.7	144.4	6658.4	19.4	6919.1
Tokyo	2.0	4.4	45.2	1905.2	3.6	1960.4

Homicide rates per 100,000 population 1981	
Philippines	34
U.S.A.	9.8
U.K.	2.4
Japan	1.5

Part 1

The overall crime rate is continuing to rise and there has been a sharp increase in violent crime, according to a report issued by the F.B.I. yesterday. The report shows that the overall crime rate for the U.S. has risen by nearly five per cent over last year. The authorities are particularly concerned about the sharp increase in the number of murders and armed robberies in large cities such as New York, Chicago and Los Angeles. It is said that black males living in New York have a one in twenty chance of being murdered, compared to the one in forty chance of death for U.S. soldiers during the Second World War. Another source of anxiety is the sharp increase in juvenile crime rates.

Reading comprehension

1 What does the report say about the overall crime rate?
2 What worries the authorities most?
3 What kind of person is life in New York the most dangerous for?
4 How dangerous is it for such people to live in New York?
5 What other kind of crime are the authorities concerned about?

Discussion

Why do you think U.S. cities have such high rates for violent crime?
Why do you think murder rates are so high for black males in New York?
Are large cities in your country dangerous? What kinds of crime are most common?
Have you ever seen or been the victim of a crime?

Part 2

Read through the list of key words and phrases before listening to the recording of a television interview. The moderator, Kay Welch, interviews Senators Charles Dryer and Henry Smith.

ban	federal law	ammunition
weapon	registered	once and for all
settlers	defend	mercy
miss the point	likely to	perfectly respectable
deprive of	pastimes	special interest groups

1 What is Senator Smith campaigning for? Why?
2 How many other developed nations allow their citizens to buy and sell guns?
3 What right does Senator Dryer want to maintain?
4 For how long has this right been recognized?
5 Why would a ban on the sale of guns reduce violent crime, according to Senator Smith?
6 Which special interest groups would oppose such a ban? Why?

Discussion

Are ordinary citizens allowed to buy and sell guns in your country?
Do you think they should be allowed to? Why (not)?
Do policemen carry guns in your country?
Do you think they should? Why (not)?

Part 3

Man Charged With Murder

Larry Hicks, a 24-year-old unemployed mechanic from Harlem, New York, was arrested yesterday and charged with the murder of a gas station proprietor. According to a police statement, Hicks tried to rob the victim as he was closing up the station for the day and when the victim resisted, he shot and killed him. He was arrested for a traffic violation a few hours later and identified as the killer from a description given by several witnesses. The murder weapon was found in his car and, after being questioned by police for some time, Hicks confessed to the crime. The prosecutor is expected to plead for the death penalty.

Role-play

In pairs take the parts of a reporter and a spokesman for the police. Ask and answer questions on:

the charge against Hicks
who he killed
why he killed him
how he was caught
how he was identified as the killer
if the murder weapon was found
if Hicks confessed to the crime
what kind of penalty he will receive

Discussion

What kind of penalty do you think this man should be given? Why?

Vocabulary

Find words in the text above which mean:

admit
owner
having no job
breach of the law relating to driving
people who saw a crime
person who was injured or killed

Guided writing

Ten different facts are given in the first sentence of the report, *Man Charged with Murder*. What are they?

Try to combine the following facts into single sentences, using the techniques used in the report.

1 A man was arrested this morning. His name is John Smith. He is 38 years old. He is a painter. He comes from Chicago. He was charged with theft. He stole a diamond. It belongs to Hilda Forest. She is a fashion designer. She is famous.

2 A woman died yesterday evening. Her name is Mildred Penn. She was 45 years old. She was a jazz singer. She came from New Orleans. She died of cancer.

Part 4
Role-playing discussion

A special commission has been set up to find ways of reducing crime in large cities. The members are lawyers and criminologists. The following proposals are to be discussed. Members will speak for or against each proposal and will then vote on which proposals to include in their final report. The proposals are:

to make penalties stricter
to introduce a mandatory death penalty for murder
to increase the number of police officers and prisons
to record the fingerprints of every citizen for storage in a central computer
to introduce moral education as a part of school curricula
to censor T.V. programs to eliminate violence

Other relevant proposals may be raised by the members.

Part 5
Language practice

Transform the following sentences as shown in the examples.

1 We should abolish the sale of guns.
   It is time we abolished the sale of guns.

   The Government should do something about crime.
   Courts should impose severe penalties.
   Parents should teach their children how to behave.
   Moral education should be introduced into the school curriculum.
   The Government should spend more money on law enforcement.
   Violent television programs should be censored.

2 People want to defend themselves so they buy guns.
   People buy guns to defend themselves with.

   I needed to pay my bills so I borrowed some money.
   He wanted to play tennis so he's trying to find a partner.
   They have to calculate their costs so they will buy a computer.
   She needed to feed her children so she stole some food.
   I want to cut my hair so I'm looking for some scissors.

3 Notice how the moderator says in the dialogue:

I believe you are campaigning . . .
I understand you do not agree . . .

In this way, he shows his willingness to be corrected if his information or impression is incorrect.
Working in pairs, make statements about each other beginning with:

I believe . . .
I understand . . .

Answer each statement with:

Yes, that's right.
No, actually . . .

4 When we apologize for something, we may say:

Excuse me for . . . ing
I'm sorry to . . .

In replying, we may say:

That's okay. (informal)
Not at all. (formal)

Apologize in the following situations, using each of the above expressions. Reply to each apology.

You interrupt someone.
Excuse me for interrupting you.
That's okay.

You are late.
You disturb someone.
You interfere with someone's work.
You are rude.
You are noisy.

16 The Third World

Farming in Southern Rwanda.

Part 1

SOMALIA REFUGEES DESPERATE

HELP HER BEFORE IT'S TOO LATE.

Half of the hundreds of thousands crowded into 32 refugee camps in the desert are believed to be children. Such is the tragedy of Somalia today. They are totally dependent on outside help − and that includes our help. Until very recently serious drought threatened their lives. Water was so short, people had to dig in dried-out river beds to get a little extra. Then heavy storms caused flash flooding. Rather than solving the refugees' problem this adds to them.

Food supplies have been damaged, trucks bogged down, and roads washed away. The shallow wells have got some days' extra water, but with so many refugees, water supplies are desperately short. Oxfam is already working in the camps. We have a medical team in the North and have now agreed to spend thousands of pounds on a major new water scheme. But money is still very short and our funds will soon run out. The refugees are desperately waiting for your help. Please send a donation today. Every penny will be used for the refugees. £5, £25 or whatever you can afford will help.

Reading comprehension

1 What is the purpose of this advertisement?
2 How will donations be spent?
3 What is the refugees' biggest problem?
4 What additional problems arose as a result of heavy storms?
5 What will happen if the refugees are not helped?
6 What exactly is Oxfam?

Role-play

In pairs, take the parts of an Oxfam relief worker and a journalist.
Ask and answer questions on:

the number of refugees
whether there are many children
why they need help
the kind of help they need
where the refugees are
how ordinary people can help
what Oxfam will do with the money
how much of it will be used for the refugees

Vocabulary

Find words or phrases in the advertisement which mean:

people fleeing from disaster
a gift
significant
not deep
lack of water
completely

Discussion

Do you feel any sympathy for these refugees? Why (not)?
Are you willing to give money to Oxfam or any other such
organization? Why (not)?
Are there similar organizations in your country?

Part 2

Read through the following key words and phrases before listening
to the recording of an interview with Dr. Paul Clark, an expert on
the problems of developing countries:

on the verge of disaster	starvation
the United Nations	crop failures
prolonged droughts	redistribute
squander	prestige
generous	the Third World

1 What kind of help do developing countries need?
2 What will happen if they do not receive such help?
3 Why are food supplies short in Africa and India?

4 What could developing countries do to help themselves?
5 What kind of projects has money been wasted on?
6 How much official aid do the rich nations give?
7 How much could they afford to give?
8 Is this aid always useful? Why (not)?
9 What kind of aid are the rich countries generous with?
10 Which countries supply most of this?

Role-play

In pairs, take the parts of Dr. Clark and a television interviewer. Ask
and answer questions on:

    the problems facing developing countries
    the cause of the food shortage
    the extent to which developing countries are to blame
    the amount of aid given by the rich countries
    if this is sufficient
    if the money is well spent
    if aid is given for other purposes
    how much military aid the countries of the Third World have
    received

Discussion

Do you think that rich countries should give aid to poor countries?
If so, why? What kind of aid? How much?
If not, why not?
Why is so much military aid given? Is it necessary?
To what extent are poor countries to blame for their own problems?
What could they do to help themselves?

Part 3

Mother Theresa, a seventy-year-old nun, was awarded the Nobel
Peace Prize in 1979 for her devotion to feeding, clothing and
housing the poor. She began her work in Calcutta in 1946 and her
order of missionaries now runs two hundred homes for the poor in
forty different countries. The following is an excerpt from a speech
she made in the U.S.A. in 1981:

"Being unwanted, unloved, uncared for, forgotten by everybody, I
think that is a much greater hunger, a much greater poverty, than
(that of) the person who has nothing to eat. I have been able to move
food to the hungry. But to the shut-ins in America and Europe, a

material thing doesn't move the loneliness. I find the hurt and loneliness a much greater disease than leprosy, T.B. or cancer, because for all these things we have medicine. For loneliness, we only have that constant touch of love. To create a relationship relieves that hunger. This is what I would like more and more people to find, to get involved in. We must find each other.''

1 Who is Mother Theresa?
2 Why was she awarded a Nobel Prize?
3 Where and when did her work begin?
4 What kind of hunger do the poor people of America and Europe suffer?
5 Why is loneliness worse than leprosy, T.B. or cancer?
6 What cure is available for loneliness?

Discussion

Mother Theresa believes that loneliness is worse than hunger or disease. Do you agree? Why (not)?
How can people who are 'unwanted, unloved, uncared for' be helped?
Who could or should help them?
What does Mother Theresa mean by, 'We must find each other'?

Guided writing

Prepare a similar advertisement to the ones on p. 91 for an organization named *Help The Poor* which is trying to collect money for victims of a famine in North Africa. Base it either on the following or on your own ideas.

Detail:
450,000 people without food or water
mostly children or old people
many suffering from disease
floods in rainy season
drought in dry season
roads unfit for motor vehicles
solution: to build dams and improve roads
cost: more than 80 million pounds

Part 4

Boronia is a small, landlocked nation with a population of 6 million people. Its only industries are agriculture and forestry although it has undeveloped mineral resources. It suffers constantly from drought and soil erosion. The World Bank has offered a grant of 2 million dollars to be used on some of the following projects:

Project	Estimated cost
a university and ten schools	$500,000
five hospitals	$500,000
wells and irrigation canals	$1m
new highways linking major cities	$1m
an airport	$1m
two luxury hotels for tourists	$1m
agricultural machinery	$500,000
reforestation project	$1m
assistance in locating and developing minerals	$1m
a bicycle factory employing 5000 people	$500,000

Role-playing discussion

You are the Ministers of Education, Health, Transport, Tourism, Finance, Industry, Forestry and Agriculture who make up the members of the Cabinet in Boronia. Discuss how the grant should be used and take a vote on it.

Part 5

Language practice

Transform the following sentences as shown in the examples.

1 We believe they are children.
   They are believed to be children.

   We think they depend on outside help.
   People say they are desperate.
   We assume they have no water.
   People report that they are dying of starvation.

2 Does this solve their problems?
   No. Rather than solving their problems, it adds to them.

   Does war reduce the number of refugees?
   Is loneliness easy to cure?
   Is the situation getting better?
   Are the unemployment figures falling?

3 Notice how *this* is emphasized below

I would like more and more people to understand this.
This is what I would like more and more people to understand.

Emphasize *this* or *that* in the following sentences.

Many people say that.
People are beginning to realize this.
She has done this for poor people.
I have been telling people this for years.
Politicians are concerned about that.

17 Industrial relations

Part 1

According to the results of a survey conducted in 1978 for the British Government, nearly half of the factories in Britain had experienced some form of industrial conflict in the previous two years and nearly one-third had experienced all-out strikes. The proportion was even higher for factories in which the workers were organized into unions with full-time shop stewards.

Conflicts between workers and management arise for various reasons. When wage negotiations break down, union officials often order a strike, a slow down or an overtime ban in order to put pressure on the management to improve their offer. In declining industries such as shipbuilding and textiles, in which layoffs are very common, workers often go on strike to protest the dismissal of laid-off employees. Less predictable and more disruptive are the so-called 'lightning strikes' (sudden strikes which begin without warning), which are often related to trivial issues like demarcation disputes, factory cafeteria prices and so on.

The frequency with which British workers resort to industrial action is probably due to two main factors: the traditionally adversary nature of industrial relations in Britain and the predominance of militant shop stewards. A typical union leader a few years ago rejected an epoch-making offer of union representation in the management of a certain large firm with the words: 'It's always been us against them and it won't work any other way.'

Reading comprehension

1 How many British factories were affected by strikes in 1976 and 1977?
2 In which factories was industrial conflict most common?
3 What kinds of industrial action often follow a breakdown in wage negotiations?
4 What is the purpose of such action?
5 In which industries are workers often laid off?
6 How do workers protest such layoffs?
7 What kinds of problems often lead to 'lightning strikes'?
8 Why do British workers resort to industrial action so frequently?
9 Why did the union leader mentioned in the last paragraph reject the company's offer?

Discussion

Do you consider going on strike to be a legitimate means of obtaining better wages and working conditions? Why (not)?
Are there any groups of workers (e.g. doctors, policemen, etc.) who should be prohibited from going on strike? If so, why?
Under what circumstances would you go on strike if you were a unionized worker?
Are strikes or other forms of industrial action common in your country? Why (not)?

Vocabulary

1 Explain the meaning of these words and phrases as they appear in the reading passage:

full-time shop stewards	slow down
overtime ban	declining industries
layoffs	demarcation disputes
adversary	epoch-making

2 Choose the words or phrases most similar in meaning to the following as used in the reading passage:

survey (a) examination (b) investigation (c) report
conflict (a) combat (b) dispute (c) trouble
break down (a) fail (b) give up (c) end
dismissal (a) retirement (b) resignation (c) layoff
predictable (a) avoidable (b) foreseeable (c) expectant
disruptive (a) confusing (b) chaotic (c) harmful to production
trivial (a) foolish (b) small (c) insignificant
predominance (a) abundance (b) power (c) great influence
militant (a) aggressive (b) violent (c) dominating

Part 2

Read through the following notes before listening to the recording of a dialogue between a union representative and a company manager:

union executive	= people who make decisions on behalf of a union
out of the question	= cannot be considered
to make ends meet	= to subsist on one's income
under-productive	= producing less than expected or required
under duress	= being forced or threatened

Listening comprehension

1 What has the union executive decided to ask for? Why?
2 Why does the manager reject their request?
3 What would happen if wages were raised? Why?
4 What are the wages of this company like compared to those paid by its competitors?
5 Under what conditions could the union's request be granted?
6 Will the union agree to help the company to increase productivity?
7 What will they do if their wage claim is rejected?
8 What would the management do if production were disrupted? Why?
9 Why can't Mr. Johnson give Mr. Evans an answer immediately?

Part 3

Role-playing discussion

Representatives of the management and labor union of a small electronics firm are engaged in negotiations. The union is demanding a twelve per cent increase in basic wage rates, longer holidays, and the cancellation of recent price increases in the factory cafeteria. The management hopes to introduce labor-saving machinery which will cause layoffs, to hold wage increases to five per cent and to introduce a quality control system. In groups, conduct appropriate negotiations using your own ideas and try to reach a satisfactory agreement.

Guided writing

> Situations Vacant
>
> International tour guide for large travel agency. Apply in writing to:
>
> The Manager, World Travel Ltd., 23, East St., London EC3

Write a letter of application for the job advertised above, giving details of:

    your present status (student, company employee, etc.)
    your qualifications and educational background

relevant experience, if any
when you will be available for interview
how you may be contacted

Begin like this:

The Manager   (your address)
World Travel Ltd.,
23, East St.,
London EC3   (date)

Dear Sir or Madam,
    I would like to apply for the position of international
tour guide if it is still . . .

End like this:
    I look forward to hearing from you.
    Yours faithfully,
            (your signature)
            (your name in printed form)

Part 4

Discussion

1 Which of these factors do you consider to be most important when choosing a job?

salary	working environment
working hours	degree of responsibility
job security	whether or not the job is easy
job satisfaction	pension
vacation	other factors (give examples)
social status	

2 Do you consider work to be:

a means of gaining enough money to live
a means of self-expression or fulfillment
an opportunity to serve society
something else

Part 5

Language practice

1 Combine the following sentences as shown in the example.

The workers were organized into unions in some factories.
In those factories the proportion was even higher.
The proportion was even higher in factories in which the workers were organized into unions.

Layoffs are very common in some industries.
In those industries, workers often go on strike.

There are militant shop stewards in some factories.
In those factories, lightning strikes are common.

Industrial relations are bad in some countries.
In those countries, productivity is falling.

Workers are more efficient in some companies.
In those companies, wages are higher.

2 Requests and demands may be refused using these expressions:

Could you lend me a thousand pounds?
I'm afraid that would be out of the question.
I've decided to use your car.
I'm afraid I can't agree to that.

Can we settle this account in instalments?
I'm sorry, but that would be impossible.

Working in pairs, make requests and demands and refuse them using the above expressions.

3 Threats are often made using the words *if* and *unless*.

If your answer isn't favorable, we'll go on strike.
Unless you increase our wages, we'll go on strike.

Make suitable threats to:
a friend who had borrowed some money from you and has not returned it
a neighbor who is having a noisy party at 2 a.m.
the manager of a factory which pollutes your neighborhood
a salesman who is pestering you
a car dealer who sold you a car which broke down the next day

18 The arms race

Military expenditure per country		
Country	% GNP	Total ($ US m)
U.S.S.R.	10.7	130,000
U.S.A.	5.6	143,974
U.K.	5.2	26,776
W. Germany	3.2	26,738
E. Germany	5.0	6,020
China	9.3	28,000
France	4.0	26,000
Israel	31.0	6,599

Source: Ruth Leger Sigard *World Military and Social Expenditures*, 1983

Part 1

In 1982, the world spent a billion dollars per day on arms. Much of this went towards increasing the existing stock of nuclear weapons. At present, there are approximately fifty thousand such weapons in the world, each capable of destroying large cities in an instant. Although only six nations have established nuclear capability, many more have the potential to build atomic weapons and some may have already done so. Among the latter group are several politically unstable developing countries which are on bad terms with each other and would probably use nuclear weapons in any future conflict. More horrifying, however, is the prospect of a nuclear war involving the major powers.

In 1962, President Kennedy threatened to destroy Russian missiles deployed in Cuba unless they were withdrawn immediately. Fortunately the missiles were withdrawn and the world was spared a nuclear war. Since then, however, both nations have modernized their nuclear arsenals and attempts to restrain the arms race have failed. The consequences of even a limited nuclear war would be disastrous not only for the protagonists but also for the rest of the world, which would be enveloped in a destructive cloud of radioactive dust.

It is hard to believe that intelligent leaders of civilized nations would allow their ideological differences to bring about the destruction of mankind, even though history teaches us not to expect leaders to be reasonable. There is, however, the frightening possibility of a nuclear war beginning by accident. On several occasions in 1980, computers employed in the U.S. defense system gave false warnings

of an attack by Soviet missiles, causing U.S. missiles to be prepared
for launching. How many times this has happened in the Soviet
Union will never be known.

While most ordinary people are indifferent to the threat of nuclear
destruction, some are actively engaged in peace movements opposed
to the arms race while others are spending their savings on fallout
shelters which, they hope, will enable them to be among the few
survivors of a nuclear war.

Reading comprehension

1 How much was spent on arms in 1982?
2 Was any of this spent on nuclear weapons?
3 How powerful are such weapons?
4 How many nations are definitely able to build such weapons?
5 Do any developing countries have nuclear weapons?
6 Who might they use them against?
7 When did the U.S. nearly go to war with the Soviet Union?
  Why?
8 How did the crisis end?
9 What would have happened if the missiles had not been
  withdrawn?
10 How would the world be affected by a limited nuclear war?
11 Is it likely that the leaders of civilized nations would allow war to
   break out?
12 Is it possible for a nuclear war to begin accidentally?
13 Why did this nearly happen in 1980?
14 Have similar incidents occurred in the Soviet Union?
15 How do most people feel about the danger of nuclear war?
16 How do some people show opposition to the arms race?
17 How do other people hope to survive a nuclear war?

Vocabulary

1 Choose the words or phrases most similar in meaning to the
  following as used in the reading passage:

arms (a) weapons (b) missiles (c) war
instant (a) while (b) moment (c) time
established (a) true (b) proven (c) supposed
terms (a) conditions (b) relations (c) times
conflict (a) argument (b) fight (c) war
prospect (a) idea (b) danger (c) expectation
spared (a) left over (b) relieved (c) saved from

arsenals (a) weapons (b) stocks of weapons (c) missile bases
consequences (a) damages (b) results (c) causes
false (a) mistaken (b) deceitful (c) misleading
indifferent to (a) the same as (b) afraid of (c) unconcerned about

2 Explain the meaning of the following words and phrases as used in the text:

such weapons	the major powers
nuclear capability	the arms race
the latter group	a limited nuclear war

Part 2

Read through the following key words and phrases before listening to the recording of an interview with an American general:

balance of power	military capacity
negotiations	verification

Listening comprehension

1 Why is it necessary to spend so much money on defense?
2 Why have negotiations on arms limitation been unsuccessful?
3 What would happen if war broke out?

Role-play

Act out this dialogue, using the above questions as a guide.

Discussion

Are you concerned about the threat of nuclear war?
What can you do to stop the arms race?
Which nations have nuclear weapons?
Which nations can produce such weapons?
Does your country have nuclear weapons?
Do you think it should have? Why (not)?
What would you do if a nuclear war broke out?
Is there any way to survive?

Part 3

On 6th August 1945, an atomic bomb was dropped on Hiroshima, a large Japanese city, killing more than 100,000 people. An observer wrote the following account.

"I was driving a truck through the outskirts of the city. Suddenly there was a blinding flash of light and my windshield shattered. A moment later, a great column of smoke rose into the sky. As I drove on towards the city center, I was stunned to find that it was in ruins. People were crawling out from the burning wreckage of their homes. They were screaming for help but there was nothing I could do. The heat was intense and I was afraid my fuel tank would catch fire so I turned around and drove away from the city as fast as I could."

Role-play

In pairs, take the parts of an interviewer and the author of the above account. Ask and answer questions on:

when the atomic bomb was dropped on Hiroshima
what the author was doing at the time
what he saw
how he felt on seeing the city center
what people were doing
if he helped them
what he did then
why he left in a hurry

Discussion

Why did the Americans drop an atomic bomb on Hiroshima?
Were they justified in doing so? Why (not)?

Guided writing

The person who wrote the above account was a truck driver. Write brief accounts which the following people might have written:

a nurse   a mechanic   a factory worker

Remember to use the past continuous form: *I was —ing . . .*

Part 4

Role-playing discussion

A nuclear war has just begun. Eight people are standing outside a nuclear fallout shelter which can accommodate only four people safely. Each person tries to persuade the official in charge of the fallout shelter to allow him to enter because of his individual merits or future value to society, while the others offer arguments against him. The eight people are:

an atomic scientist	(male) aged fifty
an injured soldier	(male) aged thirty, armed with a gun
a medical student	(male) aged twenty, who suffers from claustrophobia
a Catholic priest	(male) aged seventy
a lawyer	(female) aged thirty-five, who hates men
a pregnant heroin addict	(female) aged sixteen
an opera singer	(female) aged thirty-eight
a nurse	(female) aged twenty-five, suffering from a nervous breakdown

Part 5

Language practice

Transform the following sentences as shown in the examples.

1 A war may begin by accident.
There is the possibility of a war beginning by accident.

Computers may go wrong.
Agreements may be broken.
The other side may cheat.
The world may be destroyed.
The arms race may end in disaster.

2 I found that the city was in ruins. I was stunned.
I was stunned to find that the city was in ruins.

I heard that the war had ended. I was relieved.
I found that my house had burned down. I was shocked.
I read that my country was developing nuclear weapons. I was dismayed.
I learned that children had managed to make an atomic bomb. I was horrified.
I discovered that many people had never heard of Hiroshima. I was surprised.

3 *It is necessary to spend a lot of money on defense.*
Make sentences beginning with the following:

It is difficult to . . .	It is impossible to . . .
It is dangerous to . . .	It is easy to . . .
It is foolish to . . .	It is advisable to . . .

Text of the recordings

Unit 1

Landlord I'm sorry to have to tell you this but we've had to increase your rent by twenty-five per cent.

Tenant I'm afraid I can't agree to that. The rent's already too high. I can't possibly pay any more.

Landlord I understand how you feel but I'm afraid I must insist. You see, our maintenance costs have risen a lot over the past year.

Tenant What maintenance costs? This place is falling apart. The walls are damp and the floors are rotten. The plaster's falling from the ceiling. Are you going to repair it?

Landlord We'll be glad to discuss that once you've signed the new lease.

Tenant I'm not signing any new lease. As I told you, I can't afford to pay any more.

Landlord In that case, I'm afraid we'll have to ask you to leave at the end of the month.

Unit 2

Interviewer Is there equality of opportunity in the educational system of this country?

Commissioner It depends what you mean by "equality". Every child has an opportunity to realize his or her full potential.

Interviewer Some people feel that private education gives rich children an unfair advantage.

Commissioner It makes no difference whether one is rich or poor. Success depends entirely on one's own effort.

Interviewer It is said that private schools have smaller classes and better teachers.

Commissioner That may be true in some parts of the country. I'm afraid our budget is limited and some schools in depressed areas are below standard. But, we're doing our best to improve the situation.

Interviewer Some people feel that private schools should be abolished. What's your opinion?

Commissioner On the contrary, I believe we should encourage private education because it relieves the financial burden on the State.

Unit 3

Mrs. Randolph Mr. Preston, do you realize what will happen if these lines are closed? The roads will become even more congested. That means more traffic accidents and more pollution. Many people will move to the city and the countryside will become deserted.

Mr. Preston I admit that the closing of local lines will cause some inconvenience to a few people but it can't be helped. We can't expect taxpayers to go on subsidizing these enormous losses for ever.

Mrs. Randolph But don't you see, the rail service is an essential public amenity, the same as schools and hospitals. It shouldn't be expected to make a profit. Safe transportation of the people is the responsibility of the government.

Mr. Preston As far as inter-city services are concerned, I agree with you entirely, Mrs. Randolph. But, local transportation has to be provided by local authorities. Anyway I'm sure that every country line which is closed will be replaced by a more efficient bus service and you will have no cause for complaint.

Unit 4

Mr. West Happy birthday, Mrs. Norfolk.

Mrs. Norfolk Thank you.

Mr. West John has just told me you're eighty years old. I think it's incredible. You only look about forty. What's your secret?

Mrs. Norfolk Nothing extraordinary. Just a healthy diet and regular exercise.

Mr. West What do you eat every day?

Mrs. Norfolk For breakfast, I have granola with fruit and yogurt.

Mr. West Granola? What's that?

Mrs. Norfolk It's a mixture of cereals and nuts. For lunch, I have fresh salad and tofu.

Mr. West Excuse me? Fresh salad and what?

Mrs. Norfolk Tofu. It's a kind of curd made from soy beans.

Mr. West And what do you have for dinner?

Mrs. Norfolk Steamed vegetables and brown rice.

Mr. West Do you enjoy your meals?

Mrs. Norfolk Yes, of course. I enjoy everything in life.

Mr. West Have you ever been sick?

Mrs. Norfolk No, never.

Unit 5

Reporter Ms. Sellars, why do large firms spend so much money on advertising?

Ms. Sellars It is the best way to introduce new products to potential consumers. It is also effective in increasing sales of existing products.

Reporter It is often said that the purpose of advertising is to persuade people to buy things which they don't need. What do you think about this?

Ms. Sellars I would prefer to say that we advertisers help people to discover their latent needs. Take toothpaste, for example. Many people never realized that their social problems were caused by bad breath until they saw our commericals on T.V.

Reporter Surely many harmful products are also advertised, aren't they? Like junk food, for instance. Recently, consumers' associations have started complaining that junk-food commercials mislead the public by implying that such food is nutritious.

Ms. Sellars I would rather not comment on that. Some of our best customers are food manufacturers.

Reporter Yes, of course. Just one last question, Ms. Sellars. What are the prospects for the advertising industry over the next ten years?

Ms. Sellars I anticipate a steady increase in informational advertising and a slower increase in promotional advertising as the public becomes more and more critical of waste.

Reporter Thank you very much, Ms. Sellars.

Unit 6

Ambassador Mr. President, we are very grateful to your country. If it hadn't been for your co-operation, the incident would have ended in disaster.

President We're always glad to help our friends, Mr. Ambassador.

Ambassador My government is rather anxious that the hijacker be punished for his crime and that the money be returned.

President I'm afraid that would be out of the question. You see, the hijacker has already left the country. I'll ask our Chief of Police to give you all the details, if you like.

Ambassador I would appreciate that. Well, I won't take up any more of your time. Thank you once again for your help.

President You're welcome. Goodbye.

Ambassador Goodbye.

Unit 7

Interviewer What do you think of Concorde, Ms. Ashton?

Phillipa Ashton It's a wonderful plane.

Interviewer Why haven't any foreign airlines bought it then?

Phillipa Ashton I think the main reason is its high operational costs. It uses a lot of fuel and since the oil crisis, it has become very expensive. Also there has been a decline in the number of passengers on long distance flights.

Interviewer Why is Concorde used on so few routes?

Phillipa Ashton For one thing, not many airports are big enough to handle it. For another, many cities have refused us landing permission because their residents object to the noise made by Concorde. Moreover, some countries don't even allow us to use their airspace.

Interviewer Why not?

Phillipa Ashton They say they would suffer damage from the sonic booms, but if the truth be known, they are envious of our technological superiority, that's all.

Interviewer Is it true that Concorde flights will soon be abolished?

Phillipa Ashton There is some possibility, but no decision has been made yet.

Interviewer Thank you, Ms. Ashton.

Unit 8

Prof. Adams Ladies and gentlemen, my studies of ancient literature indicate that the sages of ancient civilization knew as much about science and astronomy as we do now. Let me give examples. According to Chinese documents, the Emperor Shun built a flying machine more than 3900 years before the Wright Brothers. In Sanskrit literature there are detailed descriptions of manned flights in India thousands of years ago.

Prof. Beck But those are only myths. They can't have built flying machines because they lacked the necessary technology.

Prof. Adams Then how could they have described them in such detail?

Prof. Court They must have had tremendous imaginations.

Prof. Adams At the time of Columbus, scientists thought the earth was flat. Yet the ancient Greeks and Indians knew that the earth was a sphere which rotated around the sun. Eratosthenes even calculated the earth's diameter accurately in about 200 B.C.

Prof. Court How did he do that?

Prof. Adams By comparing the positions of the sun at Alexandria and Syene on the same day.

Prof. Court He must have known a lot about geometry.

Prof. Adams I'm sure he did. He was in charge of the great library of Alexandria, in which much of the knowledge of the ancients was stored.

Prof. Beck What happened to the library?

Prof. Adams Unfortunately, it was destroyed.

Prof. Court Where do you think the Greeks and Indians obtained their knowledge?

Prof. Adams I believe that a great civilization existed more than 5000 years ago which was the source of all ancient knowledge.

Prof. Beck Where was it located?

Prof. Adams It may have been in Tibet; it may have been in Mesopotamia. It might even have been in Atlantis.

Prof. Court And what happened to it?

Prof. Adams I wish I knew. It seems to have disappeared without a trace.

Answers to quiz (page 46)

1 the Indian Brahmins
2 the Vikings
3 4000 years ago (in Babylon)
4 the Indian Brahmins (4320 million years)
5 the Egyptians in 2000 B.C.

Unit 9

Interviewer Dr. Ramamurti, you are said to have predicted accurately a number of events which have recently taken place. How do you manage to foretell the future with such accuracy, if you don't mind my asking?

Dr. Ramamurti There's nothing mysterious about it. You see, all events are predetermined and take place according to the relative positions of heavenly bodies. By observing the stars closely, I can anticipate certain events of great importance.

Interviewer According to current interpretations of the predictions of Nostradamus, the world is going to end in the year 1999. Do you support this theory yourself?

Dr. Ramamurti No, actually I don't. I'm far more optimistic. I believe that the final apocalypse won't take place for at least eighty years.

Interviewer So you think Nostradamus was wrong?

Dr. Ramamurti Not necessarily; but I reject current interpretations of his works. You see, Nostradamus was a mystic; he alone knew the meaning of what he wrote. Astrological predictions, on the contrary, can easily be understood by ordinary people.

Interviewer Have you yourself predicted any major events over the next ten years?

Dr. Ramamurti Yes. There will be several wars in Latin America and the Middle East. A certain well-known statesman will be assassinated. A change in climate will lead to serious food shortages in many parts of the world. These events, and many more, will be explained in detail in my next book, *What The Stars Say.*

Interviewer I look forward to reading it. Thank you very much, Dr. Ramamurti.

Unit 10

Reporter Is it true that we are facing an environmental crisis, Professor O'Sullivan?

Prof. O'Sullivan Yes, indeed. The self-generating capability of our major ecosystems has been ruined. One-tenth of all known species of plants are about to become extinct; and without oxygen, food and water, the extinction of the human race will soon follow.

Reporter What, in your opinion, has brought this situation about?

Prof. O'Sullivan One factor is the drastic increase in population over the last two hundred years. Another is the age of mass production which started with the Industrial Revolution. But I think the most significant factor is the total lack of respect shown by modern man for his environment.

Reporter Can anything be done to avert disaster?

Prof. O'Sullivan I doubt it. Even with strict control of population growth, pollution, forest clearance, and so on, complete ecological recovery would take thousands of years.

Reporter Thank you, Professor O'Sullivan.

Unit 11

Wife John, I do wish you wouldn't smoke so much. You know it's bad for your health.

Husband But it helps me relax.

Wife It may help you relax but it makes me very nervous. I think you should quit before we both get cancer.

Husband Have you forgotten what happened the last time I tried to quit? I became so irritable that you nearly divorced me.

Wife You don't have to remind me. You were terrible. Why don't you try to cut down gradually this time?

Husband I suppose I could try but I doubt if it would work.
Wife How many cigarettes do you smoke every day?
Husband About three packs.
Wife Three packs a day?
Husband Yes, it is a lot, isn't it? I suppose I could get by with two. All right, I'll try.
Wife Is that a promise?
Husband Yes, all right. It's a promise.

Unit 12

Reporter Mrs. Lloyd, I believe you have proposed several changes in the welfare system.
Mrs. Lloyd Yes, that's quite correct. The present system encourages lazy people to become parasites on society at the taxpayer's expense.
Reporter What proposals have you made?
Mrs. Lloyd Firstly, I propose a reduction in the period for which unemployment benefit is to be paid, from one year to three months.
Reporter Three months? That seems very short.
Mrs. Lloyd It's long enough for a person to find a job if he really wants one. Secondly, I propose a reduction in welfare payments. This would encourage unemployed workers to seek jobs instead of depending on welfare.
Reporter Many skilled workers who have been laid off in declining industries such as shipbuilding say they are unable to find similar jobs elsewhere.
Mrs. Lloyd They must be retrained. There are many vacancies for skilled workers in growing industries such as electronics and chemicals. I have proposed that the present industrial retraining schemes be greatly expanded.
Reporter Do you think that the changes which you have proposed would be effective in reducing unemployment?
Mrs. Lloyd Yes, definitely. They would also help to reduce taxation and increase the G.N.P. Paying idle workers for doing nothing is extremely wasteful.
Reporter Thank you, Mrs. Lloyd.

Unit 13

Interviewer How long have you been a marriage guidance counsellor, Mr. Thurber?
Mr. Thurber Over thirty years.

Interviewer You must have gained a deep insight into the problems of married couples.

Mr. Thurber I think I have, yes.

Interviewer What do you consider to be the most common problem?

Mr. Thurber Well . . . many people become disillusioned with their partners, their roles, or with marriage itself, especially in the early stages.

Interviewer What exactly do you mean by 'disillusioned'?

Mr. Thurber They start off with idealistic images of their partners and of married life. Gradually these romantic fantasies give way to cold reality as they find out their partner's weak points and start to compare their own dull lives with those of their unmarried friends. They become less willing to make concessions.

Interviewer Concessions?

Mr. Thurber Yes. Marriage involves a great deal of give and take. For the husband, this may mean sacrificing an important promotion in order to spend more time with his family; for the wife, it may take the form of accepting the tedious, soul-destroying life of a housewife. In many marriages, one or both partners find themselves unable to make these concessions and begin to blame each other.

Interviewer Is it possible to save a marriage when it has reached that stage?

Mr. Thurber Through counselling, yes.

Interviewer One last question, Mr. Thurber. Are you married?

Mr. Thurber No, not at present. My fifth wife divorced me last month . . .

Unit 14

Reporter Some experts have predicted that world production of oil will begin to decline during the next few years and that this will lead to a prolonged international recession. What are your views on this?

Prof. Watson First, they are assuming that economic growth can only be sustained by increasing energy consumption, which is not necessarily true. Consider the Japanese steel industry, for example. Energy consumption has been reduced by over 20% in the last three years while output has continued to grow steadily. As the cost of energy rises, manufacturers develop more efficient production methods. Second, it is wrong to assume oil will continue to be the major source of energy. Last year, for example, 8% of the world's electricity was generated by nuclear power plants and by 1990 that figure is expected to rise to 13%. There is enough coal to meet our energy needs for the next century. And new sources of energy are being discovered all the time.

Reporter Since you have mentioned nuclear energy, I would like to ask your opinion on this rather controversial matter. Environmentalists are strongly opposed to the construction of nuclear power plants because of the potential danger to the environment. They say that, in addition to the problem of radioactive leakage, satisfactory methods of storage and disposal of atomic waste have not yet been developed. Do you think their concern is justified?

Prof. Watson As an economist, I believe that nuclear energy has an important part to play in meeting our energy needs of the future. As a human being, however, I must confess that I find the potential hazards very disturbing. I look forward to the development of safe techniques, such as nuclear fusion, which will provide unlimited amounts of energy without producing harmful waste.

Reporter Thank you, Professor Watson.

Unit 15

Kay Welch And now let me present tonight's guests, Sen. Charles Dryer of California and Sen. Henry Smith of New York. Gentlemen, thank you very much for agreeing to appear on our show tonight. Now Sen. Smith, I believe you are campaigning for a total ban on the sale of guns.

Sen. Smith Yes, that's correct. Under present federal law there's nothing to prevent a person from selling guns and ammunition to a potential killer. Last year, nearly two thousand people were murdered in cold blood in New York City alone. In most cases, the murder weapon was a gun purchased from a registered dealer. The U.S. is the only developed nation in which citizens are allowed to buy and sell guns without restriction. It's time we abolished this evil trade once and for all.

Kay Welch Sen. Dryer, I understand you don't agree with Sen. Smith on this issue.

Sen. Dryer No, I certainly don't. Ever since the arrival of the first settlers in this country, it has been recognized that a man has the right to defend himself and his family with a gun. If ordinary citizens are prevented from buying guns to defend themselves with, they will be at the mercy of every criminal in the country.

Sen. Smith Excuse me for interrupting, senator, but I'm afraid you've missed the point. Potential criminals are far less likely to

attempt a robbery or other violent crime if they are unable to buy
guns. And ordinary people are less likely to kill each other in
anger if they are unarmed.

Sen. Dryer A large number of perfectly respectable citizens take
part in shooting and hunting for sport. They won't thank you for
depriving them of their favorite pastimes.

Sen. Smith I have no doubt that many special interest groups will
oppose this legislation; but it appears to be the only way to
prevent a complete breakdown of law and order in this country.

Kay Welch Well, I'd like to thank both of you for joining us on the
program . . .

Unit 16

Interviewer Dr. Clark, how serious are the problems facing
developing countries today?

Dr. Clark Many of them are on the verge of disaster. Millions of
people will die of starvation and disease unless the United
Nations can get food and medicine to them.

Interviewer Why has the situation become so serious?

Dr. Clark There have been a number of crop failures recently,
caused by abnormal weather conditions. Africa has been suffering
from prolonged droughts while India has experienced severe
flooding.

Interviewer Are the developing countries in any way to blame for
their own misfortunes?

Dr. Clark Yes, to a great extent. Few of them have made any effort
to control their rapid population growth or to redistribute land.
Many have squandered their precious resources on prestige
projects such as atomic power plants and colour televisions.

Interviewer What have the rich nations done to help the Third
World?

Dr. Clark Remarkably little, in my opinion. On average, they are
giving about 0.3 per cent of their GNP in official development
assistance when they could easily afford one per cent or more.
Much of this is tied to the purchase of labour-saving machinery
which causes unemployment, or of equipment which is not suited
to their technological level. The rich countries are very generous
when it comes to military aid though. Over the last twenty years,
the Third World has received 400 billion dollars in military aid,
mainly from the U.S.A. and the Soviet Union. What they need is
food and medicine, not weapons.

Unit 17

Mr. Johnson Good morning, Mr. Evans. What can I do for you?

Mr. Evans The union executive has decided to ask for a 12% increase in basic hourly wage rates in order to make up for inflation.

Mr. Johnson I'm afraid that would be out of the question. We've made hardly any profit at all this year.

Mr. Evans That's no concern of ours, Mr. Johnson. We have to take care of our families and unless our wages are raised, we'll be unable to make ends meet.

Mr. Johnson You have my sympathy of course, but you must realize that any increase in wages would raise our costs above those of our competitors and would eventually lead to the bankruptcy of this company.

Mr. Evans As a matter of fact, your competitors pay higher wages than you do.

Mr. Johnson Their wages might be slightly higher, but their workers are more productive than ours. If you help us to increase labor productivity, we'll gladly raise your wages.

Mr. Evans We're willing to discuss separately any proposals you may have for raising productivity but, I'm afraid our wage claim is not open to discussion. If your answer isn't favorable, we'll be forced to resort to industrial action.

Mr. Johnson Let me warn you that any disruption in production would cause great losses to this firm and would result in considerable layoffs of under-productive workers. I'm prepared to consider your request, but not under duress. I need several days to discuss the matter with the directors. I can probably give you an answer by next Wednesday.

Mr. Evans Very well. We can wait until then. But I doubt if we would settle for less than 12%.

Unit 18

Reporter General Fisher, this country currently spends about 5% of the GNP on defense. Is it really necessary to spend so much on arms when our country isn't involved in a war?

Gen. Fisher Definitely. We have to maintain the balance of power. As long as the Communists continue to expand their military capacity, we must do the same.

Reporter Why have negotiations to restrain the arms race been unsuccessful so far?

Gen. Fisher Neither side wants to give up the advantages it already has. There's also the problem of verification. After signing an agreement, we'd never be able to check whether or not the other side was cheating by producing new weapons secretly.

Reporter What would happen if war broke out?

Gen. Fisher We'd use all our weapons and they'd use all theirs. The human race would probably be wiped out. I hope that will never happen.

Reporter So do I! Thank you very much, General Fisher.